ANTITRUST
POLICY

ANTITRUST POLICY

The Case for Repeal

D.T. Armentano

Library of Congress Cataloging-in-Publication Data

Armentano, Dominick T.
  Antitrust policy.

  Includes bibliographical references and index.
  1. Antitrust law—United States.   I. Title.
KF1649.A84   1986   343.73'072   86-4252
ISBN 0-932790-58-5 (pbk.)   347.30372

Printed in the United States of America.

CATO INSTITUTE
224 Second Street SE
Washington, D.C. 20003

People of the same trade seldom meet together, even for merriment and diversion, but the conversation ends in a conspiracy against the public, or in some contrivance to raise prices. *It is impossible, indeed, to prevent such meetings, by any law which either could be executed, or would be consistent with liberty and justice.* But though the law cannot hinder people of the same trade from sometimes assembling together, it ought to do nothing to facilitate such assemblies; much less render them necessary.

—Adam Smith
The Wealth of Nations

Contents

Preface

Traditional antitrust policy has collapsed like a house of cards. In just 10 years—an extremely short time in matters of such importance—the antitrust regulatory authorities have gone from an enthusiastic enforcement of traditional antitrust policy in the mid-1970s to a substantial rejection of much of the conventional approach in the mid-1980s.

The recent antitrust revisionism has begun to sweep away decades of dogma concerning previous antitrust theory and practice. The standard theories of competition and monopoly developed by the economists—and traditionally held as the theoretical foundation of antitrust law—have come under severe criticism, and sharply different theories have, in some cases, been put in their place. The empirical case evidence that was said to justify vigorous enforcement of the antitrust laws has been revealed to be largely nonexistent; indeed, most of the antitrust case evidence appears directly opposed to the assumptions and conclusions of antitrust law. Finally, dozens of recent empirical investigations of various so-called monopoly-power theories have generally failed to substantiate the dire predictions of these theories. In short, massive antitrust revisionism has revealed the antitrust emperor to be wearing few, if any, clothes, and this reevaluation has rationalized some important reforms in antitrust law enforcement. It has also rationalized specific proposals for legislative reform of the laws themselves.

Several proposals for selective legislative reform have surfaced recently. Secretary of Commerce Malcolm Baldrige has called for the repeal of section 7 of the Clayton Act on the grounds that it limits mergers that domestic firms require to compete more effectively in international trade.[1] A two-year Georgetown University study of private antitrust cases suggests that treble-damage may encourage excessive private litigation and may be unjustified in some instances.[2] Finally, and most significantly, the Reagan admin-

[1]*New York Times,* November 10, 1985, pp. F1, F26.
[2]*Wall Street Journal,* November 8, 1985, p. 10.

istration has proposed a controversial five-part legislative reform of the Clayton Act.

The administration's 1986 antitrust plan is the most sweeping proposed revision of the Clayton Act in over 35 years.[3] The most innovative part of the package is a provision that would allow the president to exempt specific import-sensitive industries from any merger regulation for up to five years. The administration has taken the position that strict antitrust regulation of mergers in the past has put American firms at a competitive disadvantage vis-à-vis foreign firms. Another proposal would amend the actual language of section 7, which now can prohibit any merger that may tend to lessen competition substantially. The substitute language would prohibit only mergers in which there would be a "significant probability" that competition would be lessened. Still another proposed change would seek to severely curtail the awarding of treble damages in private antitrust cases. Finally, the administration is proposing stricter limitations on the filing of private antitrust suits against foreign firms and less strict limitations on corporate directors who sit on the boards of competing firms.

These five reform proposals are a step in the right direction, i.e., toward less antitrust regulation. As this book will make clear, government and private plantiffs have repeatedly employed the antitrust laws—including the Clayton Act—to restrict and restrain the competitive market process. Any legislative reforms that would lessen antitrust regulation generally and merger regulation in particular or inhibit a firm from filing a private antitrust suit against its competitors are entirely appropriate. Also appropriate is any attempt to exempt entire industries from section 7 jurisdiction, for any reason whatever, including the currently fashionable "threat" of international competition. Finally, stricter limitations on the awarding of treble damages will certainly cheer those who have long maintained that such awards can be both unfair and inefficient.[4]

These current proposed reforms of the Clayton Act deserve to be supported. But are these reforms sufficient? I will argue in this book that they are not. I intend to show that the case against antitrust is

---

[3]*Washington Post*, January 19, 1986, pp. H1, H4; *Wall Street Journal*, January 21, 1986, p. 28; and *Washington Post*, February 20, 1986, p. E1.

[4]For a critical examination of antitrust penalties, see Kenneth Elzinga and William Breit, *The Antitrust Penalties: A Study in Law and Economics* (New Haven: Yale University Press, 1976).

strong enough to justify the complete repeal of all of the antitrust laws.

Much is risked in a call for total repeal. Any call for repeal is likely to galvanize those interests committed to a return to the old-style, traditional enforcement policies; after all, faith in old-style antitrust enforcement has not been destroyed but simply subdued. In addition, the call for repeal would likely rekindle active opposition to the new direction in current antitrust policy. The antitrust establishment—attorneys, consultants, antitrust agency bureaucrats—would probably step up its attack on those who intend, from its perspective, to further "weaken" antitrust regulation. Critics and abolitionists would again be portrayed as pro-business and anti-consumer, devoid of concern for efficiency or fairness. The most serious danger is that a rekindled opposition could delay new and important antitrust reforms or even reverse some of the substantial administrative reforms already achieved. Why rock the boat, one might argue, when it already moves steadily in the direction of less antitrust?

Similarly, any call for repeal runs the risk of alienating the support of those critics of traditional antitrust policy most responsible for the antitrust reforms that have been achieved to this point. The majority of the important antitrust critics do not support the repeal of the antitrust laws; in their view, there is an appropriate role for antitrust policy in a free-market economy, although one that is much reduced in scope from the traditional understanding of it. Antitrust regulation, they might argue, is still important for combatting cartels and other restrictive horizontal business agreements, for example.

I disagree. There certainly are risks in working for repeal, but there are greater risks, in my view, in not pushing the intellectual argument against antitrust to its logical conclusion. I will argue that the case against antitrust regulation—any antitrust regulation—is far stronger than even its critics are willing to acknowledge. I will argue that the employment of antitrust regulation even against private horizontal agreements cannot be justified by any respectable general theory or empirical evidence. Even more practically, however, I will argue that the administrative reforms we have seen—and for which we are grateful—may only be temporary. They are, after all, only administrative reforms, and we could fall back into the quagmire of traditional antitrust enforcement. The greater risk, in my judgment (and risk assessment here is entirely subjective), would be to remain relatively content with administrative reforms while leaving the entire antitrust institutional structure of private litigation, agency enforcement, and court review essentially in place. It would be better in an entirely practical sense to abolish these institutional arrangements and be done with the greater risk.

Many of the arguments and cases that I develop here will be familiar to readers of my *Antitrust and Monopoly*.[5] New readers who find the ideas stimulating—or infuriating—may wish to pursue them in greater depth elsewhere.[6] I intend with this short book to reach a wider audience for these ideas and to promote a wider public understanding of the case against antitrust regulation.

[5]D. T. Armentano, *Antitrust and Monopoly: Anatomy of a Policy Failure* (New York: John Wiley and Sons, 1982).

[6]Yale Brozen, *Concentration, Mergers, and Public Policy* (New York: Macmillan, 1982); Fred L. Smith, Jr., "Why Not Abolish Antitrust?" *Regulation* 7 (January/February 1983): 23–28; and Frank H. Easterbrook, "The Limits of Antitrust," *Texas Law Review* 63 (August 1984): 1–40. For less radical book-length criticisms of traditional antitrust policy, see Robert H. Bork, *The Antitrust Paradox: A Policy at War with Itself* (New York: Basic Books, 1978); and Richard A. Posner, *Antitrust Law: An Economic Perspective* (Chicago: University of Chicago Press, 1976).

I. A New Direction in Antitrust Policy

Introduction

Antitrust policy has changed markedly over the last 10 years. Much of traditional antitrust enforcement has been curtailed, and a new direction in antitrust policy has emerged. In the 1980s the longstanding antitrust paranoia over the internal growth of large corporations has declined sharply. Internal business growth that tends to expand market output is now generally excluded from antitrust scrutiny. Conglomerate and vertical integration mergers—which rarely harbor any direct threat to restrict market output or reduce consumer welfare—are now of only limited concern to the antitrust authorities. Many joint-venture arrangements are permitted with little controversy, as are horizontal mergers that fall within the revised merger guidelines issued by the Department of Justice and the Federal Trade Commission in 1982. A substantial amount of price discrimination and many vertical nonprice restrictions are being perceived as part of an efficient market process, not as elements of monopoly power bent on injuring consumers. Finally, and this is important, some public and private antitrust enforcement efforts have been initiated against certain local and municipal government regulations, such as cable-television franchising and taxicab licensing, that legally restrict entry and restrain competition.

The collapse of much of the intellectual support for traditional antitrust enforcement can be traced to a number of specific developments. The most important theoretical development has probably been the increasing professional disenchantment with the so-called barriers-to-entry doctrine.[1] This doctrine held that certain economic obstacles prevented smaller companies from competing with leading firms, enhanced the market power of these leading companies, and served to harm consumer welfare. Most of these

---

[1]For an excellent criticism of the traditional barriers-to-entry doctrine, see Robert H. Bork, *The Antitrust Paradox: A Policy at War with Itself* (New York: Basic Books, 1978), chap. 16. See also Harold Demsetz, "Barriers To Entry," *American Economic Review* 72 (March 1982): 47–57.

alleged barriers have proven to be economies and efficiencies that leading firms have earned in the marketplace. Efficiency and successful product differentiation certainly can limit rivalry with firms unable to match or surpass such innovation; superior economic performance can make it difficult for new firms to enter markets or for old firms to expand their market shares. But none of this is unfair or unfortunate from any consumer perspective, and none of it can rationalize an antitrust attack on the firms with the superior performance.

A reexamination of the antitrust case evidence has also tended to support recent administrative reforms in antitrust policy. By the mid-1970s it was becoming clear that much of the antitrust case history did not confirm the resource misallocations suggested by orthodox monopoly theory. Indeed, economic analysis of the leading antitrust cases tended to demonstrate that the indicted corporations had increased their outputs and lowered their prices and had behaved generally as competitive firms would be expected to behave in open markets facing direct or potential rivalry.[2] The thrust of antitrust policy in these cases was, if anything, to restrain the competitive performance of the leading firm and thus to protect the existing market structure of generally smaller, less efficient business organizations.

These findings are perhaps best exemplified in *U.S. v. IBM*,[3] the disastrous government antitrust case against the International Business Machines Corporation that contributed significantly to the movement away from traditional antitrust policy. IBM was indicted by the Department of Justice in 1969 and charged with illegal monopolization of the general-purpose digital-computer-systems market. The suit held that IBM had systematically engaged in certain exclusionary business practices that tended to restrain trade and create a monopoly in violation of the Sherman Antitrust Act (1890). The case finally went to trial in 1975. After more than six years in court and a trial transcript of more than 104,000 pages, the case was abandoned by the government in 1982.

It was clear from the start that this government antitrust case and

---

[2]D. T. Armentano, *Antitrust and Monopoly: Anatomy of a Policy Failure* (New York: John Wiley and Sons, 1982).

[3]*United States* v. *International Business Machines Corporation*, Docket No. 69, Civ. (DNE) Southern District of New York (1969).

the many private antitrust cases against IBM[4] were all fundamentally misguided. They were, in brief, an attack on entrepreneurial success and efficiency. Clearly, IBM had not restricted production to raise prices and profits; nor had it repressed invention and innovation. On the contrary, IBM had achieved its considerable success and market share by taking unprecedented research-and-development risks, innovating superior products, and developing an unsurpassed, long-term corporate commitment to customer-support services.[5] Most of the alleged unfair practices, such as educational discounts and bundled hardware and software, were only "exclusionary" of less efficient sellers—some larger than IBM, some smaller—that could not match IBM's overall market performance.

In addition, and contrary to the assertions of the government and the private plaintiffs, IBM's considerable business success had not hurt the overall growth of non-IBM companies and the data-processing industry generally. IBM had grown rapidly, but the industry had grown far more rapidly; IBM's share of domestic electronic data processing revenues declined from 78 percent in 1952 to 33 percent in 1972, hardly persuasive evidence of any "monopolization."[6] Assistant Attorney General William Baxter understood the true state of affairs when, in 1982, his office withdrew its absurd legal action, terming it "without merit."[7]

The collapse of the "concentration doctrine" also strongly influenced the new direction in antitrust policy.[8] Early empirical work in industrial organization had appeared to discover a slight positive correlation between market concentration (the percentage of the market sales or assets "controlled" by a small group of firms, usually four) and the average profits earned by firms in such markets. Most

[4]Many companies, including Greyhound, Telex, Cal Comp., and Memorex, sued IBM under the antitrust laws. Most of these cases were resolved in IBM's favor. See Franklin M. Fisher, James W. McKie, and Richard B. Mancke, *IBM and the Data Processing Industry: An Economic History* (New York: Praeger Publishers, 1983), pp. 448–49.

[5]Franklin M. Fisher, John J. McGowan, and John E. Greenwood, *Folded, Spindled, and Mutilated: Economic Analyses and U.S. v. IBM* (Cambridge: MIT Press, 1983).

[6]Ibid., p. 111.

[7]*Wall Street Journal*, January 11, 1982, p. 3.

[8]Harold Demsetz, *The Market Concentration Doctrine*, American Enterprise Institute—Hoover Institution Policy Studies (August 1973); idem, "Industry Structure, Market Rivalry, and Public Policy," *Journal of Law and Economics* 16 (April 1973): 1–9.

of these studies assumed that the so-called barriers to entry mentioned above limited competition in the concentrated industries and allowed firms to earn monopoly profits.[9]

Later research argued, however, that the higher profits in the concentrated markets were more logically explained by the fact that the leading firms had lower costs and that these efficient firms had grown more quickly than the less efficient firms. In addition, over the long run, profit rates tended to decline in the high-concentration markets and to increase in the low-concentration markets, indicating that the competitive-market process of resource reallocation was alive and well. In short, evidence from the so-called new learning undercut much of the rationale for the traditional antitrust regulation of market concentration and high market share.[10] A new direction in antitrust policy was inevitable.

Not all traditional antitrust policies have been abandoned, however. Antitrust in the 1980s is still, for example, very much concerned with price-fixing and market-division agreements between competitors (horizontal agreements), and neither the antitrust authorities nor the courts have relaxed their position that such arrangements are normally illegal per se. In addition, certain interfirm cooperative joint ventures are still subject to regulation by the appropriate antitrust authorities. Resale price maintenance and so-called predatory practices remain illegal under the antitrust laws. The Department of Justice and the Federal Trade Commission still regulate horizontal mergers through revised merger guidelines issued in 1982. And although the merger attitudes and guidelines are somewhat more relaxed than they were in previous years, the antitrust authorities have intervened in certain steel, beer, and petroleum industry consolidations. In short, although the focus of antitrust enforcement in the 1980s has changed a little, the antitrust

[9]See, for instance, Joseph S. Bain, "Relation of Profit Rates to Industry Concentration: American Manufacturing, 1936–1940," *Quarterly Journal of Economics* 65 (August 1951): 293; and H. Michael Mann, "Seller Concentration, Barriers to Entry, and Rates of Return in Thirty Industries: 1950–1960," *Review of Economics and Statistics* 48 (August 1966): 296–307.

[10]Yale Brozen, "Concentration and Profits: Does Concentration Matter?" *Antitrust Bulletin* 19 (1974): 381–99; John R. Carter, "Collusion, Efficiency, and Antitrust," *Journal of Law and Economics* 21, no. 2 (October 1978): 434–44. An excellent discussion of the concentration and profit controversy appears in Harvey Goldschmid, H. Michael Mann, and J. Fred Weston, eds., *Industrial Concentration: The New Learning* (Boston: Little, Brown and Company, 1974).

authorities still remain active in the areas of price fixing, merger, and restrictive practices, where it is still alleged that firms are able to harm social welfare.

The progress made in moving away from the irrationalities of traditional enforcement has, by some standards, been remarkable. Critics of traditional enforcement might be tempted to be content with these important administrative changes, or even more tempted to call for some additional marginal reform, such as the general adoption of a rule of reason with respect to certain restrictive practices, for example, tying agreements or resale price-maintenance contracts. It is argued below, however, that even additional reforms cannot be sufficient and that the case against antitrust regulation is strong enough to justify the complete repeal of all of the laws.

The Case for Repeal

The case for the repeal of the antitrust laws can be summarized as follows:

First, the laws misconstrue the fundamental nature of both competition and monopoly. Competition is an open market process of discovery and adjustment, under conditions of uncertainty, that can include inter-firm rivalry as well as inter-firm cooperation. Within this competitive process, a firm's market share is not its market "power," but a reflection of its overall efficiency. Monopoly power, on the other hand, is always associated with legal, third-party restraints on either business rivalry or cooperation, not with strictly free-market activity.

Second, the history of antitrust regulation reveals that the laws have often served to shelter high-cost, inefficient firms from the lower prices and innovations of competitors. This protectionism is most obvious in private antitrust cases, in which one firm sues another, which constitute more than 90 percent of all antitrust litigation.

Third, some of the antitrust laws, such as section 2 of the Clayton Act (1914) and the Robinson-Patman Act (1936), explicitly intend to restrict price rivalry in the name of preserving competition. Government antitrust suits against firms that price discriminate almost always result in the defendant firm raising some of its prices to comply with the law.

Fourth, section 7 of the Clayton Act, which restricts mergers that may tend to lessen competition, is itself destructive of a competitive process. Restricting mergers and takeovers may inhibit the

5

flow of productive assets into the hands of more efficient managers. The anti-competitive effect of section 7 is especially evident in vertical-integration antitrust cases and in cases in which poorly performing domestic firms may require merger or other forms of cooperation in order to compete more successfully with foreign firms. Even with relaxed attitudes toward mergers and revised merger guidelines, the Antitrust Division of the Justice Department has continued to hamper important business consolidations in the domestic steel and beer industries.

For instance, the proposed 1983 merger between the LTV Corporation and Republic Steel was at first strongly opposed by the Department of Justice as violating the department's 1982 merger guidelines.[11] A proposed consolidation between U.S. Steel and National Steel was abandoned for similar reasons. When intense criticism of the merger guidelines in steel developed, the guidelines were revised to recognize that foreign steel does compete with American steel. The LTV Corporation was then permitted to acquire Republic, but not without specific divestiture-of-asset conditions.[12]

In the domestic brewing industry, many smaller regional brewers have closed their doors or sought merger partners in order to compete more effectively with industry giants Anheuser Busch and Miller Brewing. Yet public and private antitrust litigation has repeatedly frustrated brewing industry consolidation and reorganization. In 1981, for example, the aggressive Heileman Brewing Company—the nation's fourth largest brewer—was denied permission to acquire Schlitz because the Antitrust Division determined that the merger would have increased the Herfindahl Index of concentration by 128 points; Stroh, a smaller brewer, was permitted to acquire Schlitz instead.[13] Heileman's repeated attempts to purchase the Pabst Brewing Company have been similarly frustrated by both the Antitrust Division and the courts.[14] In these cases and others, arbitrary market-share calculations and Herfindahl Index numerical limits have played a determining role in both permitting and prohibiting proposed business consolidations.

[11]*New York Times*, February 16, 1984, p. D1.

[12]*Antitrust and Trade Regulation Reporter* (Bureau of National Affairs) 46, no. 1157 (March 22, 1984): 577.

[13]*New York Times*, October 22, 1981, p. 101. For discussion of the Herfindahl Index, see chapter 4.

[14]*United States* v. *G. Heileman Brewing*, 563 F. Supp. 642 (1983).

Fifth, the antitrust laws are a form of government regulation, and, like all government regulation, they tend to make the economy less efficient. In the name of preserving competition, the efficient competitive process has itself been hampered by antitrust intervention. Firms that intend to lower their prices may be restricted from doing so by antitrust law. Even more important and pernicious, firms that would innovate some new process or product must consider whether the innovation will give them an "unfair" competitive advantage or be termed "predatory" by the antitrust regulators or some competitor.

Sixth, the enforcement of the antitrust laws is predicated on the mistaken assumption that regulators and the courts can have access to information concerning social benefits, social costs, and efficiency that is simply unavailable in the absence of a spontaneous market process. Antitrust regulation is often a subtle form of industrial planning and is fully subject to the pretense-of-knowledge criticism frequently advanced against government planning.

Seventh, the antitrust laws have been enforced arbitrarily, violate traditional notions of due process of law, and always interfere with the rights of property owners or their trustees to make, or not make, voluntary agreements. As Adam Smith observed more than 200 years ago, a law that interferes with private and voluntary restraints of trade cannot be "consistent with liberty and justice."[15]

Finally, all of the considerable progress made to date in antitrust reform has been only administrative. Administrative changes and reforms are important and should not be underestimated. But they should not be overestimated, either. The antitrust statutes—even the blatantly anticonsumer Robinson-Patman Act—remain firmly in place, and some of the current enforcement effort is still traditional in nature and, therefore, thoroughly misguided.

Recent regulatory changes in the air-carrier industry illustrate the wisdom of total repeal as opposed to reform. By the mid-1970s it had become clear that government regulation of this industry, under the Civil Aeronautics Act of 1938, had worked to restrict entry, encourage wasteful practices, and raise costs and prices generally to air-transportation consumers.[16] Theoretical criticism of airline

[15]Adam Smith, *The Wealth of Nations* (1776) (New York: Modern Library, 1937), p. 128.

[16]George Douglas and James Miller, *Economic Regulation of Domestic Air Transport* (Washington: Brookings Institution, 1974).

7

regulation by economists accelerated. The empirical evidence that air-carrier regulation was inefficient and that a free market would work more efficiently became overwhelming. Theory and evidence were then cogently crafted into a solid political case for massive deregulation of the air-carrier industry.

It is important to note that the argument was not that the Civil Aeronautics Board should do less in the way of regulation or that it should do something else. The argument was that the CAB itself—the entire regulatory structure—should be abolished and an open-market process be allowed to operate in its place. The necessary and sufficient "reform" here was the total repeal of the economic regulatory structure, which occurred when Congress terminated the CAB on January 1, 1985.[17]

Air-carrier deregulation may not have worked as well had the existing regulatory structure been maintained. Deregulation often requires a painful reallocation of resources that is sure to hurt special interests, and in the air-carrier industry this process was especially painful. Strong sentiment quickly developed for reregulation, lest America lose its "national transportation system." But in the absence of any continuing regulatory structure, the general laissez-faire momentum that had been set in motion could not be reversed. As in all such cases, the results of air-carrier deregulation have been enormously beneficial to consumers.

There is an important lesson for critics of traditional antitrust policy here. Perhaps the recent administrative changes in antitrust regulation are permanent, but, given the history of antitrust policy, it is reasonable to expect that they are not. The entire regulatory antitrust structure still exists—the laws, the courts, the agencies—and this structure can be activated and employed more strictly in the future by different administrators holding different theories. The old guidelines and enforcement policies could be resumed, or an even more retrograde approach could be initiated. If the case against antitrust regulation is overwhelming, the entire antitrust framework must be abolished. A few important administrative victories must not lull antitrust critics into complacency. It would be

[17]Some of the CAB's regulatory powers, including the authority to regulate airline computer-reservations systems, were shifted to the Department of Transportation. See *Regulation* 9 (January/February 1985): 8. For the antitrust implications of DOT regulation of computer reservations systems, see *Antitrust and Trade Regulation Reporter* 48, no. 1207 (March 21, 1985): 505.

tragic, indeed, to have won most of the crucial antitrust reform battles of the last 10 years, only to lose the war at some point in the future.

Theories of Antitrust Policy

It will not be easy to repeal the antitrust system. Antitrust regulation is a firmly entrenched institution in America and has been since 1890. This section explores some of the reasons for the persistent faith in antitrust regulation—despite its record—and speculates on the more subtle meaning of antitrust.

Antitrust as Public Interest

The primary reason for the widespread support for antitrust enforcement is a belief that the laws still serve, however imperfectly, to protect the economy (consumers) from the economic abuses commonly associated with private monopoly and private-monopoly power. This perspective can be termed the "public interest" theory of antitrust policy.

The notion of competition is enormously popular in American society. We expect and enjoy competition in sports and in business. In business, competition is said to keep organizations alert and efficient. Business competition gives consumers quality products at low prices, provides buyers with alternative suppliers, forces poorly managed firms out of the market, and limits and restricts so-called economic power.

Monopoly appears as the antithesis to all of this. Business monopoly is said to deaden initiative and efficiency, restrict production, raise prices, exclude competitors from the market, and misallocate economic resources. It can be economically and even politically dangerous. It is a short step from these impressions to supporting a law that encourages competition and prohibits business monopoly—that is, an antitrust law.

Academic economists have crafted these impressions concerning competition and monopoly into an elaborate theoretical paradigm that serves to legitimize some antitrust regulation. Put briefly, this theory holds that free markets can occasionally fail to work in the best interests of society generally. This so-called market failure can occur whenever private business organizations gain monopoly power, the power to restrict production and raise market price. Such firms can produce less and charge more, and they generally have higher costs than comparably competitive business organizations. A law

9

that prohibits free-market monopolization would appear to promote increased outputs, lower costs, and lower prices for consumers. Antitrust law, therefore, exists to protect the public interest from the power of free-market monopoly.

There are at least two ways to analyze this public interest perspective on antitrust policy. One way is to challenge the theoretical models of competition and monopoly upon which it is so heavily dependent. If the models are fundamentally deficient, then the scientific case for antitrust is weakened substantially. The other way to challenge the public interest perspective is to study the actual conduct and performance of business organizations that have been convicted under the antitrust laws. If such firms were found not to be restricting production and raising prices—if, indeed, they have been increasing outputs and lowering prices—then the public interest theory of antitrust regulation would be all but demolished.

Antitrust as Regulation

An entirely different perspective on antitrust policy is to see it as an example of special-interest regulation. Government regulation in America has often been associated with special-interest groups, usually business groups, that have attempted to use legislation to gain and hold economic advantages (or "rents") not obtainable in a free market.[18] These advantages are often secured by legal barriers to entry and competition that serve to restrict production and increase prices. The recent system of "voluntary" import quotas in the automobile industry, for example, has had the effect of protecting domestic auto companies from foreign competition while inflicting massive economic losses on consumers.[19]

Antitrust, despite disclaimers, is government regulation. Whether antitrust was originally intended to promote and protect special business interests can never be known with absolute certainty,

---

[18]George J. Stigler, "The Theory of Economic Regulation," *Bell Journal of Economics and Management Science* 2 (Spring 1971): 3–21; Sam Peltzman, "Toward a More General Theory of Regulation," *Journal of Law and Economics* 19 (August 1976): 211–40. For a review of the rent-seeking literature, see Robert D. Tollison, "Rent Seeking: A Survey," *Kyklos* 35 (1982): 575–602.

[19]See *A Review of Recent Developments in the United States Automobile Industry, Including an Assessment of the Japanese Voluntary Restraint Agreement* (Washington: International Trade Commission, February 1985). See also Robert W. Crandall, "Import Quotas and the Automobile Industry: The Costs of Protectionism," *Brookings Review* 2 (Summer 1984): 8–16.

although there is some evidence that such may have been the case.[20] But, as will be demonstrated below, there is adequate evidence that antitrust has often been employed as special-interest legislation. In practice, antitrust has been protective of existing market structures—much like tariff and quota protection—and has served to keep costs and prices higher to final consumers. Antitrust defendants have lost cases because their efficient performance—low prices and successful innovations—has been ruled "exclusionary" of less efficient competitors. In private cases, especially, antitrust has often been employed as a club by plaintiff firms anxious to restrain the price and innovational rivalry emanating from efficient defendant corporations. And since private cases constitute more than 90 percent of all antitrust litigation, they are revealing of the fundamental nature of antitrust policy.[21] In short, antitrust, like almost all government regulation, has often served to benefit some at the general expense, a result fully anticipated by much of the public choice literature.[22]

If this perspective on antitrust regulation is correct, antitrust law will actually be harder, not easier, to repeal—or even to additionally reform. The social costs of such special-interest legislation as antitrust are normally spread very thinly over society as a whole; consider for example, the per capita costs of nonsense cases such as the 13-year government war on IBM or the recent FTC crusade against the leading ready-to-eat cereal companies. Yet the benefits of antitrust regulation are frequently concentrated on very special interests—the antitrust establishment—and those benefits can be substantial. Antitrust attorneys, private plaintiffs, consultants, and the antitrust bureaucracy itself have much to gain from a continuation of antitrust regulations and much to lose from any repeal of or reduction in antitrust enforcement. Consequently, the beneficiary groups have every incentive to strenuously resist reform and

[20]Thomas J. DiLorenzo of George Mason University has recently shown that outputs in the "trust" industries—far from being restricted—expanded rapidly in the decade prior to the Sherman Act of 1890. He has also argued that Sen. John Sherman's motives in sponsoring the act may have been ambiguous. See Thomas J. DiLorenzo, "The Origins of Antitrust: An Interest-Group Perspective," *International Review of Law and Economics* 5 (1985): 73–90.

[21]See, for example, Betty Bock et al., *Antitrust in the Competitive World of the 1980's*, Conference Board Research Bulletin no. 112 (1982), pp. 18–19.

[22]See, for instance, Robert D. Tollison, "Public Choice and Antitrust," *Cato Journal* 4, no. 3 (Winter 1985): 905–16.

11

repeal and to denounce all antitrust critics in the most strident tones. Ordinary citizens and consumers, on the other hand, have little incentive to rally against the antitrust juggernaut, little incentive even to educate themselves as to the antitrust facts of life. This cost-benefit calculus makes any attempt to repeal the antitrust laws difficult, unless that calculus can be changed.

Antitrust as Industrial Policy

A third perspective on antitrust policy is to see it as one of America's oldest industrial policies. Industrial policy is government industrial planning, and antitrust policy is a kind of government planning. For example, the Justice Department and the FTC have published detailed merger guidelines that proscribe legally permissible business consolidations. Indeed, they often intervene in mergers, even while permitting them, requiring that firms sell certain assets or companies. The 1984 merger of Texaco and Getty was FTC-approved pending the sale of 600 service stations, certain pipelines, and several refineries; the Gulf-Chevron merger was FTC-approved after an agreement was reached to sell 4,000 Gulf stations and a major oil refinery.[23]

Further examples of antitrust industrial policy include the FTC's authority to review the costs and benefits of joint business ventures, such as the Toyota-GM joint venture, and to grant or deny approval of inter-firm cooperative agreements. The antitrust authorities can move against firms that fix resale prices, charge low (predatory) prices, charge high (monopoly) prices, and charge prices that are the same (collusion). The Justice Department can decide that rate bureaus in the trucking industry are inappropriate under certain circumstances, even though they have been in general use for decades.

This point about industrial planning and policy is emphasized not to quibble over labels but to point out that antitrust, like other government-planning policies, is subject to criticism on the grounds that it always assumes the existence of the information it requires for intelligent decisions concerning social efficiency. As will be argued later, the cost-benefit information that would be required for intelligent choices concerning mergers and divestitures is pro-

---

[23]*Oil and Gas Journal*, January 23, 1984, p. 48; *Oil and Gas Journal*, February 6, 1984, p. 84; *Oil and Gas Journal*, July 16, 1984, p. 43; *Wall Street Journal*, April 24, 1984, p. 4.

duced and discovered only through a working out of the open market process and is knowable only to the particular individuals involved in that process. Antitrust authorities and courts continually presume the existence of such information when they prohibit a merger, deny a joint venture, break up a company, or rule that certain prices are predatory. Yet, if antitrust regulators and courts cannot obtain accurate information concerning future social costs and benefits, no rule of reason in antitrust is really possible. The case against antitrust regulation is thus all the stronger.

Those who argue that antitrust is not government industrial planning will have difficulty explaining the recent decision to break up the American Telephone and Telegraph Company, probably the most significant employment of antitrust regulation in the history of antitrust enforcement. This historic consent decree, among other things, divested the 22 operating telephone companies from AT&T and ended a portion of a 1956 consent decree that had prevented AT&T from competing in nonregulated markets, such as data processing.[24] Ending the 1956 consent decree—a legal restriction on market entry and competition—was entirely consistent with permitting a spontaneous market process to exist in telecommunications and data processing. Divesting the operating companies and reorganizing them into seven regional companies was, however, an unprecedented experiment in antitrust industrial planning.

A number of economic arguments were employed to justify the divestiture of the operating telephone companies. The first was that AT&T's ownership of the operating companies served as a bottleneck to potential long-distance competitors. AT&T's ownership of the operating companies, so the argument went, placed it in a position to deny the "competitors" fair access to the bulk of the business and residential telephone market. The second argument was that divestiture would reduce the potential threat of cross-subsidization of revenues from regulated markets to unregulated markets and end the necessity of restricting AT&T from entering unregulated markets. Finally, the divestiture would serve to weaken the grip of AT&T's Western Electric Company on the telephone-equipment market (since the operating companies had ordered the bulk of their equipment from Western), leading to additional innovation and lower equipment prices.

[24]*United States* v. *AT&T*, 524 F. Supp. 1336 (1981); *United States* v. *AT&T*, 552 F. Supp. 131 (1982).

These arguments are not entirely implausible, and the AT&T divestiture may lead to the results anticipated. But how do its supporters know that the assumed, future benefits of divestiture will exceed its costs? For example, even Robert W. Crandall and Bruce M. Owen, in their excellent discussion of the divestiture issues, concede that the absence of any direct evidence on AT&T's pre-divestiture vertical-integration joint economies makes it "very difficult to prove that the divestiture is necessarily welfare enhancing."[25]

Indeed, most consumer difficulties in telecommunications do not relate directly to vertical integration and divestiture at all; government regulation, not vertical integration per se, has been the primary obstacle to a truly open-market competitive process in telecommunications. The Federal Communications Commission has long restricted entry into long-distance telecommunications and has regulated the rates of the monopoly supplier, AT&T. Entry into local telephone markets has been legally restricted by state governments, and phone service and rates have been regulated by public utility authorities; the dominant supplier is, again, AT&T. This regulation is not, of course, accidental. AT&T has a long history of advocating government regulation and monopoly in telecommunications and of opposing attempts to increase competition by decreasing government regulation.

Most of the alleged difficulties associated with AT&T's vertical integration—and most of the alleged benefits associated with divestiture—are difficulties that could have been overcome in time by complete deregulation. Cross-subsidization, for instance, becomes a serious issue only in a regulated setting where a firm might choose, say, to finance price-cutting wars in unregulated markets out of revenues or profits earned in regulated markets. Ending the regulation ends the possibility of "unfair" cross-subsidization. In addition, Western Electric's near capture of the operating-company market for telephone equipment is controversial only because the operating companies can pass along, under regulation, all of the inflated equipment costs to the final consumer of phone services. In an openly competitive market, consistent noncompetitive purchases of materials by vertically integrated companies would nor-

[25]Robert W. Crandall and Bruce M. Owen, "The Marketplace: Economic Implications of Divestiture" in *Disconnecting Bell: The Impact of the AT&T Divestiture*, ed. Harry M. Shooshan (New York: Pergamon Press, 1984), p. 57.

mally result in a severe loss of market share for those companies—a strong incentive to change the practice. Again, it is regulation, not vertical integration, that is the ultimate source of the difficulty.

Even the so-called bottleneck and access issues are forever clouded by the fact that, under divestiture, no open-market access value exists for the rival long-distance companies. The current access fees are not market determined but are set under the authority of the FCC. In the absence of true market values, even supporters of divestiture cannot be sure that the existence of rival suppliers will actually improve overall resource efficiency and advance the elusive public interest.[26]

Conclusions

Very little academic or public credence is given to antitrust policy as special-interest regulation or as government industrial planning. Government regulation and planning have been sharply criticized by economists and, by and large, have been professionally discredited.[27] What support now remains for antitrust policy would appear to depend upon the public interest perspective, that is, the belief that some antitrust regulation is necessary to prevent market failure.

In the following chapters, the public interest theory of antitrust will be critically examined to determine whether the standard theories of competition and monopoly employed to explain market failure actually make sense and whether the classic antitrust cases contain evidence that free-market monopoly can exist and misallocate resources. If antitrust theory and history are internally consistent, then some antitrust policy may be appropriate. If, however, they are inconsistent, then the public interest perspective and the policy it supports deserve to be rejected, not simply reformed. Without a scientific public interest justification, there is no rationale for any antitrust regulation in a market economy.

[26]There is increasing evidence that the "public interest" has not been advanced by the divestiture. See Paul W. MacAvoy and Kenneth Robinson, "Losing by Judicial Policymaking: The First Year of the AT&T Divestiture," *Yale Journal on Regulation* 2 (1985): 225–62.

[27]See, for example, Robert W. Poole, Jr., ed., *Instead of Regulation* (Lexington, Mass.: Lexington Books, 1983). An excellent critical analysis of the entire government-planning paradigm by many authors can be found in *Cato Journal* 4, no. 2 (Fall 1984). For a definitive book-length criticism of government planning see Don Lavoie, *National Economic Planning: What Is Left?* (Cambridge, Mass.: Ballinger, 1985).

II. Competition and Monopoly: Theory and Evidence

Much of the support for antitrust policy depends upon the correctness of the standard theories of competition and monopoly. These can be briefly summarized as follows.

The Theories

Some economists define "competition" as a state of affairs in which rival sellers of some homogeneous product are so small—relative to the total market supply—that they individually have no control over the market price of the product.[1] These atomistic sellers take the market price as given and then attempt to generate an output that maximizes their own profit. The final outcome (equilibrium) of such a market organization of firms is that consumers obtain the product at the lowest possible cost and price. Such markets are said to be "purely" competitive ("perfectly" competitive if there is perfect information), and resources are said to be allocated efficiently.

Free-market monopoly involves some voluntary restriction of market output relative to the output forthcoming under competitive conditions. Economists usually assume that "monopoly" means that there is only one supplier of a product with no reasonable substitutes or that several major suppliers of a product collude to restrict production. The economic effect of such monopolization is that market outputs are restricted—the monopoly "restrains" trade—and prices are increased to consumers. Such restrictions of production are also said to misallocate resources and reduce social welfare.

The expression "misallocation of resources" is a powerful one in economics. It signifies that scarce economic resources are not being put to their greatest economic advantage. The implication is that

---

[1] The standard theoretical analysis of competition, monopoly, and resource misallocation can be found in any microeconomics text and in most texts on antitrust policy. See, for instance, Peter Asch, *Industrial Organization and Antitrust Policy* (New York: John Wiley and Sons, 1983), chap. 1.

some alternative allocation of these resources could improve overall economic performance.

Monopoly is said to misallocate resources in two fundamental ways. The first is termed "allocative inefficiency." It implies that the price consumers pay for a product under monopoly—the monopoly price—exceeds the marginal cost of producing that product. Consumers indicate their willingness to have suppliers produce more of some product by paying a price that exceeds the marginal cost of producing it. Firms with monopoly power, however, can maximize their profits by restricting their production and keeping their prices up. Suppliers with monopoly power are said to have no incentive to expand production to the point where market price and marginal cost are equal. The consequence of such supply decisions is that resources are at least somewhat misallocated and social welfare is reduced.

Monopolists are also said to be likely to expend resources to obtain monopoly positions and then expend additional resources to retain them. Further, in the absence of direct seller rivalry, monopoly suppliers can afford to be less efficient than competitive firms with respect to their own use of resources. All of these extra expenses and inefficiencies can increase the cost function under monopoly relative to competition and contribute to what is termed "technical inefficiency." In short, firms with monopoly power can produce less, charge more, and misallocate economic resources. Society would be clearly better off under conditions of competition, and the rationale for antitrust enforcement against monopoly is said to be obvious.

The Problem with Competition Theory

Although the standard theories of competition and monopoly seem reasonable and would appear to rationalize some antitrust enforcement, they pose some very serious difficulties. Resource allocation under atomistic competition might well be efficient if perfect information existed or if tastes and preferences never changed, but it is difficult to understand the relevance of such a theory in a real world of differentiated preferences, economic uncertainty, and dynamic change. The economic problem to be solved by competition is emphatically not one of how resources would be allocated if information were perfect and consumer tastes constant; with everything known and constant, the solution to a resource-allocation problem would be trivial. Rather, the economic problem lies in

18

understanding how the competitive market process of discovery and adjustment works to coordinate anticipated demand with supply in a world of imperfect information. To assume away divergent expectations and change, therefore, is to assume away all the real problems associated with competition and the resource-allocation process. Thus, although the standard efficiency criteria may be technically correct for a static world, they are irrelevant to actual market situations.

Market uncertainty and change may require differentiated products. They may also require some inter-firm coordination, instead of independent rivalry, and even some price cooperation. They may require some product and service advertising, although none is required in the atomistic equilibrium. These variables do not indicate that competition does not exist or that the competitive process is defective or inefficient. They mean, simply, that the competitive process is in a necessary state of disequilibrium. The market process may, in the abstract, tend toward some theoretical equilibrium, but it never reaches one.

Much of traditional antitrust enforcement has been based on erroneous notions of efficiency under static equilibrium conditions. Outputs falling short of the purely competitive—theoretical—output were said to have been "restricted." Market advertising, product differentiation, and innovation were often said to be elements of monopoly power—not elements of a competitive process—that could misallocate resources and lower social efficiency. Any control over market price was termed monopoly power, and inter-firm cooperative agreements were regarded by economists and the antitrust authorities with great suspicion. Yet, if purely competitive equilibrium is not an appropriate welfare benchmark, none of these traditional conclusions make any sense.

An alternative perspective on competition is to see it as an entrepreneurial process of discovery and adjustment under conditions of uncertainty.[2] A competitive process implies that business organizations of various sizes continually strive to discover which products and services consumers desire, and at what prices, and contin-

---

[2]F. A. Hayek, "The Meaning of Competition," in *Individualism and Economic Order* (Chicago: Henry Regnery Company, 1972), pp. 92–106. On the historical development of the distinction between the competitive process and the competitive equilibrium, see Paul J. McNulty, "Economic Theory and the Meaning of Competition," *Quarterly Journal of Economics* 82 (November 1968): 639–56.

ually strive to supply those products and services at a profit to themselves and at the lowest cost.

This process of discovery and adjustment may encompass explicitly rivalrous behavior in the usual sense—direct price and nonprice competition—and it may also include various degrees of inter-firm cooperation, such as joint ventures and mergers, as well. Inter-firm cooperation and rivalry are not opposing paradigms from a market-process perspective. There is no a priori way, for example, to define the optimal size of a cooperative business unit or, alternatively, the optimal number of rival firms for efficient market coordination. Even price agreements between firms may serve to reduce risk and uncertainty—during a recession, for example—and lead to an increase in market efficiency. (See chapter 4.) Cooperation and rivalry are alternative institutional arrangements by which entrepreneurs, under conditions of uncertainty, strive to discover opportunities and coordinate plans in a continuous search for profits. Public policy should not hinder the development, or collapse, of these arrangements.

In competition, profits and losses serve to provide the necessary information and incentive for continuous entrepreneurial alertness. Some business organizations may be more successful than others in this process and may earn significant market share; other organizations may do poorly, lose market share, and even fail. Both the growth and decline of companies is a necessary part of the discovery procedure. Finally, while individual markets may tend to clear during this process, error and changing information, among other things, must prevent the realization of any final equilibrium condition.

The Problem with Free-Market Monopoly Theory

Similar theoretical difficulties discredit free-market monopoly theory as well. The primary one concerns the actual ability of a monopoly firm, or a group of colluding firms, to restrict the market supply and realize monopoly prices and profits. Although a firm may intend to restrict market supply and garner monopoly profits, the ability of free-market monopoly to achieve that result is questionable.

The standard textbook treatment often assumes a monopoly output restriction and then proceeds to compare that restricted output, unfavorably, with an atomistic equilibrium output level.[3] But both

---

[3]See, for instance, Edwin Mansfield, *Microeconomics: Theory and Applications*, 5th

the assumption and the comparison are entirely misleading, for the atomistic equilibrium output level is neither possible nor relevant and cannot serve as the welfare benchmark for any comparison. Moreover, it is difficult to understand how any output level that is inefficient or generates substantial profits can be sustained in an open market in the face of strong incentives to expand production.

Free-market monopoly power created through merger or collusion is presumably the primary concern of the antitrust authorities. But if the economic effect of monopolization is to raise prices above costs—marginal and average—strong economic incentives then exist to expand current production and to encourage output by new firms. If production increases, prices will fall and the market will tend, other things being equal, toward a situation in which prices and costs are equal.

What happens if a free-market monopolist attempts to subvert this competitive process and discourage rivalrous entry by lowering prices? The reduced prices would induce additional sales, and the market situation would then tend toward the traditional competitive equilibrium. What happens if a monopolist discriminates in price? Indeed, there might be strong economic incentives to do so, but a monopolist that price discriminates will end up selling additional output at some lower price, and, again, the market will tend toward the traditional competitive output. Certainly a monopolist that is inefficient cannot deter market entry; inefficiency will act as an invitation to entry and additional output. On the other hand, a monopolist that is clearly more efficient than potential rivals can deter entry, but it would be the efficiency of the monopolist that would keep competitors out. Resources are not misallocated and the competitive process is not subverted when high-cost firms are restrained from entering markets by the superior product or efficiency of existing suppliers.

Firms may intend to restrict market output through collusion and cartel agreements, but the realization would be even more tenuous than that possible through a one-firm monopoly. Not only would a cartel of suppliers encounter the same incentives to expand production reviewed above, it would also face such difficulties as coor-

ed. (New York: W. W. Norton, 1985), p. 294. The entire notion of a free-market monopoly price and output may be untenable. See Murray N. Rothbard, *Man, Economy, and State: Volume 2* (Princeton: D. Van Nostrand Company, 1962), pp. 604–15.

dinating and policing its own supply-restriction schemes.[4] Inter-firm agreements to restrict rivalry could exist in a free market, as they did occasionally under common law prior to the Sherman Act, and they might even be able to temporarily stabilize some price fluctuations, but there is little reliable evidence that free-market collusion can allow conspiring firms to capture monopoly profits.[5] Moreover, inter-firm cooperation may well have significant benefits that could overwhelm any possible negative output restriction. (See discussion in chapter 5.)

Likewise, the usual textbook discussions of inefficiency under monopoly are unconvincing. The standard argument of allocative inefficiency is, in fact, contrived and misleading. With new entry and output blocked by definition, a monopolist is said to misallocate economic resources relative to their allocation under conditions of pure competition. But this "misallocation" occurs only because the competitive process is assumed to be ended in atomistic competition (price, marginal cost, and minimum average cost are all assumed to be equal) and because *no competitive market process is allowed to begin under monopoly.* If, on the other hand, a competitive process always does operate under free-market monopoly, and if it is assumed that no final atomistic equilibrium condition can ever exist, then resource misallocation under free-market monopoly, as some unique social problem, simply disappears. Allocative inefficiency would tend to disappear from the free-market monopoly model, just as it would tend to disappear from the competitive disequilibrium model, and for exactly the same reasons.

Also debatable are the standard assumptions concerning technical inefficiency under monopoly. In any serious attempt to monopolize some free market, businesses are far more likely to lower costs than they are to raise them, and to expand rather than decrease production. The most effective way to gain and hold a free-market monopoly position is to be more efficient than rivals or potential rivals. In addition, larger firms may simply have lower costs than smaller firms, due to scale economies associated with

[4]The difficulties of effective collusion are reviewed in D. T. Armentano, *Antitrust and Monopoly: Anatomy of a Policy Failure* (New York: John Wiley and Sons, 1982), pp. 133–37. See also George J. Stigler, "A Theory of Oligopoly," *Journal of Political Economy* 72, no. 11 (February 1964): 44–61.

[5]A negative relationship between collusion and profitability is found by Peter Asch and Roberta Seneca in "Is Collusion Profitable?" *Review of Economics and Statistics* 58 (February 1976): 1–12.

manufacturing, financing, and marketing, or due to innovation. Thus, overall business costs are just as likely to be lower, not higher, as firms seek a monopoly position in a free market. (By contrast, the costs of obtaining and securing legal monopoly are socially wasteful; this matter is discussed below.)

Occasionally the issue of technical inefficiency is confused by allowing the costs of product differentiation to slip into an analysis of increased costs under monopoly. Firms producing differentiated products often incur extra costs, and these costs are sometimes compared unfavorably with the costs incurred by firms under conditions of atomistic competition. But this comparison is not valid, for once goods are differentiated, their costs cannot be compared directly with the costs of homogeneous goods. That consumers choose to pay higher prices to cover the higher costs of differentiated products proves nothing about inefficiency or waste, nor does it misallocate resources. (See chapter 3.)

In summary, the legitimacy of antitrust regulation in the public interest must depend upon a reasonably sound theory of how free-market monopoly can continue to restrict production and increase prices and how it can make the economy less efficient and misallocate resources. Yet, as has been argued here, the standard theoretical approach suffers from serious shortcomings. In the first place, monopoly output is often compared with an impossible atomistic output, hardly a meaningful comparison. In addition, it is difficult to understand how free-market monopoly power can continue to restrict production and sustain prices while allowing firms to earn monopoly profits. (Barriers to entry, including so-called predatory practices, will be discussed in chapter 3.) The inefficiencies alleged to exist under free-market monopoly are, similarly, either contrived or irrelevant. In short, *all* firms in free markets are engaged in a competitive market process. Standard free-market monopoly theory cannot support its own conclusions in any reasonable fashion, much less support government antitrust intervention into private markets in the so-called public interest.

The Evidence

There are two fundamental kinds of evidence concerning monopoly. The first is case-study evidence, much of it taken from classic antitrust cases. The *Standard Oil* antitrust case of 1911[6]—perhaps

---

[6]*Standard Oil Company of New Jersey* v. *United States*, 221, U.S. 1 (1911).

the most famous and misunderstood anti-monopoly case in all of business history—illustrates the difficulties associated with free-market monopoly theory.

The conventional account of the *Standard Oil* case goes something like this. The Standard Oil Company employed ruthless business practices to monopolize the petroleum industry in the 19th century. After achieving its monopoly, Standard reduced market output and raised the market price of kerosene, the industry's major product. The federal government indicted Standard under the Sherman Act at the very pinnacle of its monopolistic power, proved in court that it had acted unreasonably toward consumers and competitors, and obtained a divestiture of the company that helped to restore competition in the petroleum industry.

This account has almost nothing in common with the actual facts. It is not possible to review the entire history of the case here, but a summary of the government findings against and actual conduct of Standard Oil will serve to make the point.

The Standard Oil Company was a major force in the development of the petroleum industry in the 19th century. Standard grew from being a small Ohio corporation in 1870, with perhaps a 4 percent market share, to become a giant, multidivisional conglomerate company by 1890, when it enjoyed as much as 85 percent of the domestic petroleum refining market. This growth was the result of shrewd bargaining for crude oil, intelligent investments in research and development, rebates from railroads, strict financial accounting, vertical and horizontal integration to realize specific efficiencies, investments in tank cars and pipe lines to more effectively control the transportation of crude oil and refined product, and a host of other managerial innovations. Internally generated efficiency allowed the company to purchase other businesses and manage additional assets with the same commitment to efficiency and even to expand its corporate operations abroad.

Standard Oil's efficiency made the company extremely successful: it kept its costs low and was able to sell more and more of its refined product, usually at a lower and lower price, in the open marketplace.[7] Prices for kerosene fell from 30 cents a gallon in 1869 to 9 cents in 1880, 7.4 cents in 1890, and 5.9 cents in 1897. Most important, this feat was accomplished in a market open to competitors, the number and organizational size of which increased greatly

[7]See Armentano, pp. 55–73.

24

after 1890. Indeed, competitors grew so quickly in the years preceding the federal antitrust case that Standard's market share in petroleum refining declined from roughly 85 percent in 1890 to 64 percent in 1911. In 1911, at least 147 refining companies were competing with Standard, including such large firms as Gulf, Texaco, Union, Pure, Associated Oil and Gas, and Shell.

This rivalrous development is not surprising, given the enormous changes in the petroleum industry that took place after 1890. Standard Oil, which had dominated the Pennsylvania crude-oil markets and the national manufacture of kerosene, had its market position challenged by the development of crude-oil production in the southwestern United States and by a product demand shift away from kerosene. The increasing popularity of fuel oil, and eventually gasoline, and Standard's inability to control the market availability of crude (Standard itself produced only 9 percent of the nation's supply in 1907) practically guaranteed that the petroleum industry would not be monopolized by any one business organization.

Conventional wisdom holds that the government antitrust suit against Standard proved that the firm had reduced outputs and increased prices and employed ruthless business practices toward its suppliers and competitors. But the facts are otherwise. The lower-court judges who convicted Standard in 1909 found only that the formation of its holding company Standard Oil of New Jersey in 1899 was a "contract or combination in restraint of trade," forbidden explicitly by the Sherman Antitrust Act.[8] Dissolution of that company was held to be the appropriate—and sufficient—judicial remedy to restore competition.

This fact is extremely important. The lower court did not find that prices for kerosene were higher because Standard had reduced outputs or that the rebates it had secured from the railroads were unfair. The lower court did not rule on any of the substantive economic issues—although it had, of course, heard the government's argument and Standard's defense on various charges.

It is also generally assumed that, since the famous *Standard Oil* decision of 1911 established the "rule of reason" principle, the Supreme Court must have applied it to Standard's business practices and determined that it had indeed restrained market output and raised market price. It is true that Justice White, writing for a unanimous court, argued that the rule of reason had existed under

[8]*United States* v. *Standard Oil Company of New Jersey*, 173, F. Rep. 179 (1909).

the common law and ought to be employed in antitrust cases. And it is true that White wrote that "no reasonable mind" could but conclude that Standard had, indeed, acted unreasonably under this legal principle.

But it is emphatically not true that the High Court presented any specific finding of guilt with respect to the charges of misconduct and monopolistic performance brought by the government. That sort of determination is the job of a lower or trial court anyway, and, as already noted, the trial court had found Standard guilty of no specific illegality with respect to the important substantive issues. All that the Supreme Court did—contrary to overwhelming conventional wisdom—was conclude that some of Standard's practices, such as merger, evidenced an unmistakable intent to monopolize and that these practices were unreasonable. Why were they unreasonable? Because the Court said that it was obvious that they were. Certainly no detailed analysis of Standard's market performance—as would be common practice in subsequent rule-of-reason monopoly cases—was ever conducted by either the trial court or the Supreme Court.

Since subsequent research has shown that petroleum outputs expanded and prices declined throughout the 19th century and that Standard had not engaged in ruthless business practices, like predatory price cutting, the *Standard Oil* case can hardly be cited by antitrust enthusiasts as evidence that monopoly is a free-market problem or that antitrust is necessary to protect the consuming public from private economic power.

The second kind of evidence concerning monopoly consists of empirical studies of market concentration, profitability, and the so-called welfare losses associated with monopoly power. In these studies, profitability often serves as the measure of monopoly power and resource misallocation.

The thinking behind profitability as the measure of monopoly power is that economic profits would tend to be dispersed under competitive conditions; hence, the existence of economic profits in the long run could be an indication that the competitive process has been restricted. Some empirical studies argue that certain business expenses, such as advertising and even product differentiation, should be included with profits in any measurement of the overall social costs associated with monopoly power.[9]

9There have been various attempts to measure the social cost of monopoly. See,

There are, however, some very serious methodological difficulties associated with these studies, including the concentration-profit studies discussed earlier.[10] In the first place, most empirical studies use accounting profit data to draw conclusions about economic profit—a debatable procedure at best. Second, legal monopoly and free-market monopoly might well be inexorably intertwined in the actual business world: tariffs, quotas, licensing, and other legal restrictions always tend to generate economic rents in markets that are otherwise openly competitive. Third, empirical studies almost always take the atomistically competitive equilibrium condition as a welfare benchmark. While economic profits might well be dispersed in some imaginary equilibrium world, that is irrelevant in any actual resource-allocation problem. Profits (and losses) are always essential in providing the information and incentives required to ensure that resources are being allocated from less valuable uses to more valuable uses. Long-run profits may imply that some organizations are relatively more efficient than others over long periods of time and that the competitive process has not yet reached any final equilibrium.

Such economic factors as uncertainty, risk, price expectations, and innovation are not short-run market disturbances that disappear if only we wait long enough. They are a continuous part of the competitive market process. Moreover, advertising and product differentiation in a disequilibrium world cannot simply be treated as some unwelcome welfare burden or social cost. (See chapter 3.) In short, profits need not evidence any extraordinary social inefficiency or burden; nor can empirical regression studies of profit and concentration ever serve as a reliable guide for rational antitrust regulation.

Legal Monopoly and Consumer Welfare

While free-market monopoly theory is seriously flawed, it is true that legal barriers to competition can create resource-misallocating monopoly power. Government, usually at the behest of some

---

for example, Keith Cowling and Dennis C. Mueller, "The Social Cost of Monopoly Power," *Economic Journal* 88 (December 1978): 727–48.

[10]For an excellent criticism of all such studies and measurements, see S. C. Littlechild, "Misleading Calculations of the Social Costs of Monopoly Power," *Economic Journal* 91 (June 1981): 348–63. For a statistical criticism of concentration-profit studies see Eugene M. Singer, *Antitrust Economics and Legal Analysis* (Columbus, Ohio: Grid Publishing, 1981), pp. 31–33.

industrial interest, may decide to legally restrict entry into certain markets. Government licensing, certificates of public convenience, legal franchise, and quotas both foreign and domestic—each can tend to restrict entry, reduce the supply of available output, or raise the market price of a product to consumers. Firms and suppliers that would have voluntarily entered into trade and exchange with willing consumer-buyers are legally prevented from doing so; consumers who would have willingly purchased additional output at lower prices cannot; and innovations that would have been introduced by new suppliers are delayed or lost altogether. The competitive market process has been undercut and artificially short-circuited—by law.

The government power of monopoly—of legally restraining trade—can have the effect of reducing market supply and raising market price. This restriction of output is not voluntary; nor is it due to "disequilibrium." There has been no voluntary refusal to deal or trade; prospective buyers and sellers are, presumably, anxious to trade and thereby to improve their relative welfare, but they are prevented from doing so by law. Potential suppliers are not excluded because they are less efficient users of capital or cannot realize economies of scale; they are excluded arbitrarily by government power. Indeed, a reasonable guess is that some of the potential entrants are more efficient than existing producers—else why the necessity of legal restrictions?

Moreover, there are no economic incentives that tend to offset legal output reductions. The economic incentives for protected business organizations are, as explained earlier, to maintain or expand existing monopoly restrictions that legally exclude potential competitors. Firms will waste additional resources to retain legal privileges and their monopoly rents. Indeed, all of the conventional criticisms of monopoly actually do apply to legal monopoly and rationalize the repeal of such restrictions.

Conclusions

This chapter has argued that the theory of free-market monopoly is flawed. Neither theory nor evidence can rationalize antitrust policy. But if legal barriers restrain trade, can antitrust regulation be justifiably used against them?

Employing antitrust against legal barriers to entry enacted by state and local governments may create incentives to dismantle those barriers. In fact, antitrust critics are often entirely sympathetic to using antitrust in an already regulated society solely to remove legal restrictions on competition or cooperation.[11] Some important caveats are in order, however. First, employing antitrust against legal barriers to entry is the only application of antitrust that can be rationalized. Second, the possible dangers from antitrust misuse—prosecuting cooperative agreements between suppliers instead of strictly legal barriers to trade, for example, and the continuation of private antitrust—are likely to be so great as to overwhelm the marginal benefits that could arise from prosecuting legal monopoly. If the political choice were to retain antitrust regulation or abolish it completely, total abolition would still be the better course. Finally, should Congress or the courts move to block further the application of antitrust to legal monopolies, there would again be no rationalization for any antitrust policy.[12]

[11]See D. T. Armentano, "Towards a Rational Antitrust Policy," hearings before the Joint Economic Committee, November 14, 1983, in *Antitrust Policy and Competition* (Washington: Government Printing Office, 1984), pp. 23–33.

[12]The so-called *Parker* doctrine (*Parker* v. *Brown*, 317 U.S. 341 [1943]) already makes explicitly authorized state-government regulation exempt from antitrust law. The Local Government Antitrust Act of 1984 eliminates personal antitrust liability for municipal officials. See *Antitrust and Trade Regulation Reporter* 47, no. 1178 (August 16, 1984): 345–52.

III. Barriers to Entry

The logic of free-market monopoly theory is said to be enhanced by a discussion of nonlegal barriers to entry. Although open markets contain no legal barriers by definition, certain nonlegal obstacles are alleged to exist that may hamper the competitive process and allow leading firms to misallocate resources. Presumably, the application of antitrust policy against these barriers increases economic efficiency and consumer welfare.

Product Differentiation

Antitrust enthusiasts argue that the extra costs associated with product differentiation tend to restrict market entry.[1] Firms that would like to enter, say, the automobile industry, understand that they must incur such costs as retooling for annual body-style changes, and these costs can deter entry. If the product were homogeneous, especially homogeneous over time, it would be far cheaper to enter the auto market and, accordingly, there would be more rivals.

Differentiation is also alleged to be an element of monopoly power. Firms that successfully differentiate their products are said to be able to raise their prices above the level possible in a "purely competitive" market.[2] Thus, although there may well be intense rivalry among sellers in markets where products are differentiated, the competition is said to be "imperfect," and resources are still said to be somewhat misallocated.

These arguments are unconvincing. If products have been successfully differentiated—that is, if consumers have expressed a willingness to cover the costs associated with differentiation—then the difficulty of entering markets and competing with established firms relates directly to those revealed consumer preferences. If buyers of automobiles have traditionally supported annual body-

---

[1]Joseph S. Bain, *Barriers to New Competition* (Cambridge: Harvard University Press, 1956); and idem, *Industrial Organization* (New York: John Wiley and Sons, 1968).

[2]See, for example, the discussion in Phillip Areeda, *Antitrust Analysis: Problems, Text, Cases*, 2d ed. (Boston: Little, Brown and Company, 1974), pp. 17–23.

style changes and punished firms that did not make them, then clearly it is consumer preferences that have helped limit rivalrous entry into the automobile industry.

While this development might be a problem for particular would-be suppliers, it is not a problem for consumer welfare generally or for efficient resource allocation. Efficient resource use implies that resources should be put to the uses that consumers, not economists, value most highly. If consumers support annual body-style changes, *that* is the use to which resources should be put. Potential or existing competitors can always attempt to convince consumers to support less product differentiation—at a lower price—or perhaps no year-to-year differentiation at all. Alternatively, potential entrants can always attempt to discover cheaper methods of production and marketing that would allow rivalry with established firms. But, in the absence of such preference changes or discoveries, potential competitors are indeed restricted from production by the performance of rivals and the revealed preferences of consumers. These restrictions are not, however, barriers to entry that can rationalize antitrust intervention.

From the perspective of antitrust critics, it is entirely appropriate that efficiency and revealed preferences should limit entry and exclude potential rivals, for resources are scarce and have alternative uses. The economic problem is to ensure that scarce resources are put to their highest consumer-valued use and reallocated from less valuable to more valuable uses—which is precisely the social function of the competitive market process. Competition is not restricted by efficiency and consumer choice.

The essential confusion—and it recurs often in antitrust economics—is over the meaning of the term "competition." If competition means the purely competitive equilibrium, then competition can be inappropriately restricted by product differentiation and producer efficiency. But, as already argued, pure competition cannot be an appropriate welfare standard in antitrust: it is a static equilibrium condition with no competitive process. It assumes homogeneous products and preferences, the existence of suppliers already employing the best technology, and the absence of error or surprise. Resources are efficiently allocated in such a world, but only because the model simply assumes the conditions required for an equilibrium.

The actual competitive process is one of discovery and adjustment; it is not a static state of affairs.[3] The economic problem is not one of allocating resources efficiently when everything is known and constant, but of learning how to allocate and reallocate resources in an uncertain and changing world. Competition is an entrepreneurial process of discovering what, in fact, consumers do prefer and which firms, employing which technologies and strategies, will be able to supply those products. The competitive process is not restricted by the failure of specific products or firms; nor is it limited because efficiency and preferences prevent some would-be rivals from competing. Those who say they are preserving competition by preserving specific competitors or by subsidizing new firms to enter markets do not understand the purpose of a competitive market process.

Some critics of differentiation assert that some product differentiation is essentially frivolous, involving no real improvements.[4] But how are "real" improvements to be distinguished from "cosmetic" changes, if not by the revealed preferences of consumers? Critics are entitled to their opinions on these issues, but consumers in a free market have the final word on whether differentiation is "worth it" or not. If consumers believe that an "improvement" is frivolous, they will not be willing to pay much for it. On the other hand, if they are willing to pay substantially more for some differentiation, then it is demonstrably not frivolous and the resources it uses are not misallocated.

Firms can, of course, make errors and miscalculate consumer preferences. They can underestimate or overestimate the value that consumers are likely to place on any differentiation or some innovation. They can expend resources in the present only to discover in the future that they cannot recover those expenses. In such situations, resources have in some sense been wasted.

But this use of the term "waste" must be put in the context of the economic problem that is to be solved in a market economy. Part of the problem is that firms attempt to coordinate their supply decisions with the preferences of consumers before consumers

[3]Israel Kirzner, *Competition and Entrepreneurship* (Chicago: University of Chicago Press, 1973).

[4]See, for example, the discussion in Ralph T. Byrns and Gerald W. Stone, *Economics*, rev. ed. (Glenview, Ill.: Scott, Foresman and Company, 1984), p. 607. See also Willard F. Mueller, "The Anti-Antitrust Movement," in *Industrial Organization, Antitrust, and Public Policy*, ed. John V. Craven (Boston: Kluwer-Nijhoff Publishing, 1983), pp. 30–31.

actually reveal their preferences in the marketplace. Firms must correctly anticipate the revealed preferences of both consumers and competitors, and this anticipatory process is filled with risk and uncertainty. Importantly, the problem of plan coordination involves not only price coordination—which most primary economics texts dwell on exclusively—but also product coordination: the product must be precisely the one that consumers prefer. Thus both price and product must be coordinated before any market can be efficient from a consumer perspective.

Many discussions of competition trivialize this coordination problem by assuming that perfect information concerning consumer tastes and prices already exists or that the market has somehow already selected some standardized product for sale. But this assumption is unrealistic. In actual market situations, firms discover product prices and preferences only through a working out of the competitive market process itself. While there are very strong economic incentives for firms to anticipate consumer preferences and the plans of competitors correctly, resource-allocation mistakes—given the fundamental uncertainty involved—are inevitable. Markets cannot be expected to work perfectly, to realize perfect equilibrium or coordination. All that can be reasonably expected is that the free-market process will tend toward an efficient solution by continually creating information and incentives to reallocate resources from less valuable to more valuable consumer-determined ends.

The recent Federal Trade Commission case against the leading ready-to-eat (RTE) cereal companies is an excellent example of the antitrust confusion over product differentiation, consumer preferences, and barriers to entry.

In 1972 the FTC brought suit against Kellogg, General Foods, General Mills, and Quaker Oats, arguing that the firms' 90 percent market share constituted a monopoly in the RTE cereals industry.[5] The leading companies competed by proliferating new brands of cereal and variations of old brands; they rarely engaged in direct price competition. According to the FTC, the market-share position of the firms was a direct function of this "wasteful" brand proliferation, which had the effect of severely restricting new-firm entry and competition. The costs and risks associated with developing, producing, and marketing a new cereal brand were generally pro-

[5]In the Matter of Kellogg Company, General Mills, Inc., General Foods Corporation, the Quaker Oats Company, FTC Docket No. 8883, complaint issued April 26, 1972.

hibitive for new companies. In addition, the lack of price competition allowed the leading companies to earn "excessive" profits over a long period of time. The solution, according to the FTC, was to break up the leading companies and force them to license their popular trademark brand names out to would-be rivals.

The FTC is no doubt correct in concluding that the high risk of failure in producing new cereal brands limited market entry. It is also true that certain economies associated with size, especially in advertising, tended to restrict the number of new competitors. But it is not true that any of this is regrettable from any consumer perspective, or that the competitive process was endangered, or that these restrictions can justify any remedial antitrust activity.

Efficiency in the use of resources, including efficiency in the specific types of products produced, can always restrict the number of competitors. As has been argued, the very purpose of the competitive market process is to discover which products consumers prefer, for whatever reason, and then to produce and sell those products to consumers. The fact that leading firms with long experience and economies of scale may be able to accomplish this task more efficiently than smaller or newer organizations is irrelevant from a consumer perspective: consumer welfare is not injured thereby and resources are not misallocated.

The issues can be put another way. If cereal-brand proliferation had been unsuccessful from a consumer viewpoint, the larger companies would have lost market share to other companies and would no longer have been the leading firms in the industry. If cereal costs for the larger companies had been higher—not lower—than for their would-be competitors, the larger firms could have lost market share to smaller, more efficient companies and, again, would not have remained leading firms. In short, if the larger RTE firms had not been efficient and successful with their products, they could not have remained the leaders in their industry for decades.

The fact that the leading companies had introduced dozens of new cereal brands successfully in an uncertain market setting is direct evidence of sustained efficiency in the use of resources, not evidence of monopoly power that misallocated economic resources. Consumers were not coerced into purchasing new cereal brands; they were invited to try them. Consumers were not overcharged for differentiated cereal products; they willingly paid more for new brands of cereal they perceived to be more valuable than old brands. Rival manufacturers or would-be competitors who believed this behavior to be irrational on the part of consumers were always free to test their theory of efficient cereal marketing. If consumers really preferred less differentiated cereal brands at lower prices, then the newer or smaller firms would have been able to compete easily.

Actually, the FTC's successful attempt in the late 1970s to drop the Quaker Oats Company from the original antitrust complaint undermined its entire theory concerning barriers to entry in this case. Quaker Oats had, in fact, accomplished precisely what the FTC had argued was nearly impossible: it had innovated important new products and brands and had increased its market share in an industry dominated by larger companies. Quaker had developed a line of so-called natural cereals and persuaded consumers to purchase them, thereby breaking the tight grip of the leading companies on the market. Despite the Quaker Oats episode, the FTC continued to pursue the case—only to lose in 1981 before an administrative judge and then before the full FTC in 1982.

Advertising

Advertising is likewise often criticized as a barrier to entry that limits competition and causes resources to be misallocated. In the academic economist's perfectly competitive model, there is no advertising since products are assumed to be homogeneous and market information on products and prices is assumed to be perfect. In the real world of differentiated products and ignorance, however, economists have had to account for the appearance of product advertising. Some conclude that advertising allows firms to differentiate products and then charge higher prices for them, and that large advertising budgets can enable large companies to sustain their market share at the expense of smaller rivals and potential entrants. Others argue that, in the absence of perfect information, advertising allows a more efficient plan coordination process between suppliers and consumers by lowering information and search costs. The first group of economists tends to see advertising as an element of monopoly power that generates some social inefficiency;[6] the second, as an element of a competitive process that allows an

---

[6]Joan Robinson, *The Economics of Imperfect Competition*, 2d ed. (New York: St. Martin's Press, 1961). See also the discussion in Douglas F. Greer, *Industrial Organization and Public Policy* (New York: Macmillan, 1980), pp. 44–84.

understanding of how resources are efficiently allocated in an uncertain world.[7]

Since the issue of product differentiation as a barrier to entry has already been discussed, that analysis need not be repeated here. It might be noted, however, that the treatment of advertising by some critics as a superfluous selling expense—as distinguished from other, legitimate production and transportation costs—is totally arbitrary. All business costs are selling costs in the sense that all resources are expended with the purpose of selling products to consumers at a profit. Advertising costs, in this respect, are no different from quality-control costs, tool costs, fire-insurance costs, or any other expenditure made to accomplish some potentially profitable activity. In perfect competition with perfect information, advertising would be unnecessary (so would fire insurance!), but that is irrelevant to the problems that must be solved in a dynamic and uncertain market economy.

It is true, however, that some business organizations perform advertising functions more efficiently than rival firms. Some even achieve substantial economies of scale through effective advertising, earning higher profits as well. These earned efficiencies can be a barrier for less efficient firms, but, again, there is no misallocation of resources. The only obvious waste here is on the part of the firms that advertise less effectively.

But can successful firms earn long-run monopoly returns on their advertising investments? Some early empirical studies appeared to discover a positive relationship between advertising expenditures and firm profitability, and that led some corporate critics to conclude that advertising could generate excessive returns.[8] More recent studies, however, which have treated advertising expenditures as an investment rather than as a current business expense, have failed to substantiate any adverse advertising-profit association.[9]

[7]Philip Nelson, "Advertising as Information," *Journal of Political Economy* 82 (July–August 1974): 729–54; Yale Brozen, "Entry Barriers: Advertising and Product Differentiation," in *Industrial Concentration: The New Learning*, ed. Harvey Goldschmid, H. Michael Mann, and J. Fred Weston (Boston: Little, Brown and Company, 1974), pp. 115–37.

[8]See, for example, William S. Comanor and Thomas A. Wilson, "Advertising, Market Structure, and Performance," *Review of Economics and Statistics* 49 (November 1967): 423–40.

[9]Robert Ayanian, "Advertising and Rate of Return," *Journal of Law and Economics* 18 (October 1975): 479–506; Harry Bloch, "Advertising and Profitability: A Reappraisal," *Journal of Political Economy* 82 (April 1974): 267–86.

Even if such a statistical association did exist, it would prove nothing sinister. There is no requirement that the competitive business world conform to the economist's notion of a long-run equilibrium condition where all market anomalies have been eliminated and all firms are earning the same return. Certainly, there may well be strong tendencies toward an equilibrium condition in an open market, and a notion of equilibration and coordination underlies much of our understanding of an efficient competitive process. But again, long-run business equilibriums are not possible and thus cannot be the relevant benchmark to appraise the market performance of competitive firms.

Efficiency

It can be admitted readily that economies and efficiencies achieved by some firms but not by others can delay and even prevent entry and direct market rivalry. Firms that enjoy economies of scale or some low-cost technology do make market rivalry more difficult or, in the extreme case, even impossible. If it were correct from a market perspective to argue that more competitors are always better than less, then economies of scale might be condemned out of hand for restricting competition.

But clearly that is not the correct analysis. The exclusions associated with efficiency are appropriate because it is the consumers who ultimately decide to support efficient and penalize less efficient firms. Again, the purpose of the market process is to discover the efficient service, the efficient product, the efficient business organization; competition—both rivalry and cooperation—has nothing to do with some arbitrary number of firms. If consumers want more competitors, they can have them by demonstrating their willingness to pay the higher prices necessary to cover the costs of less efficient or new competitors. Most of the time consumers are unwilling to do so. Certainly, consumer decisions not to support additional competitors are not inefficient; nor do they reduce consumer welfare. Antitrust regulation is not necessary to save consumers from themselves.

The Aluminum Company of America prior to 1937 is a classic example of a near business monopoly maintained essentially through innovation and industrial efficiency as a barrier to entry. In the lower-court antitrust case decided in favor of Alcoa in 1939,[10] Judge

[10]The lower-court decision is *United States* v. *Aluminum Company of America*, 44 F.Supp. 97 (1939). The appeals-court decision is *United States* v. *Aluminum Company of America*, 148 F. 2nd. 416 (1945).

Caffey laboriously determined that Alcoa had not monopolized bauxite (contrary to what many textbooks still report), waterpower sites, alumina, or aluminum castings, wire, and other aluminum products. The firm had not illegally monopolized the production of aluminum ingot. Nor had it charged exorbitant prices or earned exorbitant profits. Prices for aluminum ingot—Alcoa's primary product—declined from approximately $5 per pound in 1887, the year Alcoa was founded as the Pittsburgh Reduction Company, to 22 cents per pound in 1937, the year Alcoa was indicted for monopolization. During that period, profits averaged approximately 10 percent on overall investment. Nor had Alcoa engaged in any illegal exclusion of potential competitors. The only so-called preemptive purchase of a potential competitor was a Justice Department–approved purchase of a failing French firm in 1915. Given these findings, Judge Caffey dismissed the entire antitrust complaint against Alcoa.

Alcoa had been the only domestic supplier of virgin ingot aluminum for 50 years, even though the patents on the electrolysis process for making aluminum had expired in 1906. Entry into primary aluminum production had proved difficult—even to potential entrants like Henry Ford—because Alcoa enjoyed vast scale economies in production and technological advantages in research and development. Furthermore, Alcoa passed along these economic advantages to buyers in the form of competitive ingot prices, forestalling competitive entry by behaving as if there indeed were potential rival ingot sellers anxious to steal Alcoa's customers and overwhelming market share. Only as a consequence of such superior economic performance did Alcoa hold a "monopoly" market share in virgin ingot.

The lower court had made an important distinction between being "a monopoly" and "monopolizing" in restraint of trade. For Judge Caffey, being a monopoly—absent any unfair exclusionary practices—was reasonable and not a violation of the Sherman Act, which did not condemn monopoly per se. A business might achieve a monopoly position by, for example, being more efficient than its rivals, and the law was not intended to condemn such situations.

The appeals court that reversed Judge Caffey's decision and decided against Alcoa in 1945 also agreed that Alcoa had been efficient. But Judge Hand, breaking with the rule of reason, determined that Alcoa's "skill, energy, and initiative" had excluded competition and that efficiency was not a legal excuse for monopolization. He wrote in his decision:

> It was not inevitable that it [Alcoa] should always anticipate increases in the demand for ingot and be prepared to supply them. Nothing compelled it to keep doubling and redoubling its capacity before others entered the field. It insists that it never excluded competitors; but we can think of no more effective exclusion than progressively to embrace each new opportunity as it opened, and to face every newcomer with new capacity already geared into a great organization, having the advantage of experience, trade connections and the elite of personnel.[11]

Alcoa's competitive strengths actually sealed the antitrust case against it. If the company had been less efficient, presumably, there would have been more "competition," i.e., competitors, and no violation of the law. Such is the twisted economic logic of antitrust in the *Alcoa* case.

Actually there were competitors, although the appeals court in 1945 steadfastly refused to recognize them. Hundreds of rival firms sold what is termed "secondary aluminum," or scrap aluminum ingot, which was then a near-perfect—and hence competitive—substitute for Alcoa's own primary ingot. If one includes the sale of secondary ingot, Alcoa's share of the relevant market dropped from 90 percent (the remaining 10 percent share going to aluminum imports) to 66 percent—and then, with other reasonable adjustments, to 33 percent. Alcoa was not even monopolizing any reasonably defined relevant market.

Capital

It is sometimes held that financial capital can be a barrier to competitive entry and can allow leading firms to monopolize. Some would-be producers, the argument goes, must pay a higher price for capital than already established businesses.

All scarce resources have prices that must be paid in order to allocate (or reallocate) them to higher-valued uses. Financial capital, like all resources, cannot be free to all who would want to use it, and its costs must be borne by those who intend to employ it productively.

The explicit cost of capital is determined in competitive capital

---

[11]*United States* v. *Aluminum Company of America*, 148 F. 2nd., pp. 430–31.

markets, and firms that would purchase it must do so at freely determined market prices. Some firms are able to acquire capital at lower prices because their demonstrated risks for using capital effectively are lower. A firm in business for more than 50 years, with a continuous record of profitable returns on its investments, will likely have lower capital costs than some new firm with little experience employing capital successfully.

Thus capital costs can be a barrier to entry. More efficient users of capital will tend, all else being equal, to exclude less efficient users of capital from the market. But efficiency as a barrier is hardly unfair to or injurious of consumer welfare. Indeed, such a barrier— and the exclusionary process it implies—is absolutely essential to ensure that scarce capital flows to those firms most likely to employ it profitably in the service of consumers. Since thousands of new firms do obtain capital and do eventually succeed and expand, this so-called barrier to competition can be overcome like all other non-legal barriers—by superior economic performance. And that, from the perspective of consumer welfare, is exactly the way that it should be. The only rationale for government policy here would be to eliminate any legal barriers that might restrict buyer or seller access to debt or equity markets.

Predatory Practices

"Predatory price cutting" implies that leading firms can price their products in ways that adversely affect rivalry or potential rivalry. Firms might, for example, temporarily price below cost in an attempt to eliminate rivals or discourage potential entry into markets. "Nonprice predatory practices" implies that leading firms can employ some nonprice competitive variable—such as a product innovation or advertising—in ways that raise a competitor's costs or render the demand for a competitor's product or service obsolete. In the watch industry, for instance, some leading firm might suddenly introduce a revolutionary new watch that tends to make the demand for the watches of smaller competitors obsolete. The effect of this innovation, it is alleged, might be to reduce competition substantially and harm consumer welfare.

Although the word "predation" sounds antisocial, there are important difficulties with any attempt to use antitrust policy to restrain such rivalrous behavior. In the first place, how are the regulators and the courts to distinguish truly predatory practices from the normal price reductions and exclusions that occur during any competitive market process? Are prices below money costs always predatory? And which costs are relevant for such determinations? Average costs? Marginal costs? Long-run marginal costs? Why are historical accounting costs relevant at all? Although there has been an extensive discussion (some would say too extensive) of some of these questions in the professional journals over the years, no clear answers have emerged.[12]

Even if economists could agree on what is meant by predatory pricing, it is still not obvious why such pricing behavior should be legally restricted. After all, predatory practices cannot succeed without direct consumer-buyer support. For example, if prospective buyers ignore a leading firm's price reductions, then those reductions clearly cannot be predatory. On the other hand, if buyers alter their preferences and support the price cutter, it is the buyers—not the price cutter—that put pressure on the high-price firms and may ultimately eliminate some of them. Consumer-buyers can always eliminate certain competitors by altering their buying preferences and choosing one product, for whatever reason, over another. There is no reason for antitrust to interfere in this process.

Antitrust enthusiasts might argue that buyer choices to reward the price cutter are not in the long-run interests of buyers. But no one can know the long-run interests of buyers. Furthermore, the superiority of so-called long-run interests to short-run interests cannot be assumed. Buyers can surely decide their own time preferences and then decide whether the advantages of short-run price reductions exceed the possible disadvantages of fewer suppliers in the future. Consumer choices are rational either way, and consumer welfare is reduced only when government antitrust policy prevents consumers from determining the market-supply structure they apparently do prefer.

The same argument holds with respect to nonprice predatory practices; indeed, the relevant issues are exactly the same. If a leading firm introduces some product innovation, it is up to consumers to decide whether the innovation will reduce the number of competitors. If consumers enthusiastically support the innovation at the expense of competitive products, then some rival sup-

[12]See, for example, Phillip Areeda and Donald Turner, "Predatory Pricing and Related Practices under Section 2 of the Sherman Act," *Harvard Law Review* 88 (February 1975): 697–733; and Oliver E. Williamson, "Predatory Practices: A Strategic and Welfare Analysis," *Yale Law Journal* 87 (December 1977): 284–340.

pliers may well be eliminated. On the other hand, if consumers do not support the innovation, the innovation cannot threaten competition and cannot be predatory. In neither scenario is there a legitimate rationale for regulatory preferences superseding the revealed preferences of buyers with respect to the pace and nature of technological change. Indeed, it would be difficult to imagine an antitrust intervention as potentially dangerous or damaging to future consumer welfare as this sort of innovation regulation.[13]

Some economists, notably John McGee, have argued that predatory practices are not normally rational or efficient ways of gaining or holding market share.[14] Firms that engage in predatory pricing, for instance, stand to lose a considerable amount of revenue, and profit, in funding a predatory "war." If the firm is large and the war is long, the costs and risks are sure to create substantial disincentives to engage in it. In addition, target competitors may not be easily driven from business, or, even if they are, their assets may be acquired by new firms willing to compete as soon as the predatory price is lifted. In short, considerable financial risks are associated with price predation, and such risks may create powerful disincentives to engage in it, especially in industries with no legal barriers to entry.

There are very few unambiguous examples in business history of leading firms attempting to secure, or hold, near-monopoly positions by engaging in extensive predatory practices.[15] Even the allegedly classic examples of predatory practices in the 19th-century petroleum and tobacco industries, involving Standard Oil and American Tobacco, are either exaggerated or unfounded. Standard Oil, as already argued, secured its market position in petroleum primarily through internal efficiency and merger, not systematic predatory practices. And while the American Tobacco Company may have occasionally employed severe price competition to gain market share—the great "snuff war" comes to mind—no general predatory policy would have been intelligent in an industry like tobacco, where there were thousands of competitive suppliers and

[13]For a discussion of the antitrust attack on innovation, see Betty Bock, *The Innovator as an Antitrust Target*, Conference Board Information Bulletin no. 174 (1980).

[14]John S. McGee, "Predatory Price Cutting: The Standard Oil (N.J.) Case," *Journal of Law and Economics* 1 (October 1958): 137–69.

[15]Ronald H. Koller, "The Myth of Predatory Pricing: An Empirical Study," *Antitrust Law and Economics Review* 4, no. 4 (Summer 1971): 105–23.

no barriers to market entry.[16] Even when such pricing wars did occur in the tobacco industry, consumers enjoyed them immensely by purchasing greatly increased amounts of tobacco products at very low prices—for years. There is no obvious reason why antitrust regulation should restrain such occasional practices that clearly benefit consumers.

Conclusions

The purpose of this discussion has been to argue that nonlegal barriers to entry cannot rationally support free-market monopoly theory or justify antitrust intervention. Business experience, economies of scale, advertising efficiencies, successful product innovation, and dozens of other competitive advantages that business organizations earn may well inhibit the entry of would-be suppliers, but such limitations and exclusions are not inefficient, do not injure consumers, and—correctly understood—do not reduce competition in the marketplace.

[16]D. T. Armentano, *Antitrust and Monopoly: Anatomy of a Policy Failure* (New York: John Wiley and Sons, 1982), pp. 85–95.

IV. Price Discrimination and Vertical Agreements

The antitrust laws still forbid price discrimination and vertical business agreements (merger, resale price maintenance) that may tend to reduce competition substantially. Price discrimination can be illegal under section 2 of the Clayton Act (1914) as amended by the Robinson-Patman Act (1936). Mergers can be illegal under section 7 of the Clayton Act. Tying contracts and other restrictive agreements can be illegal under section 3 of the Clayton Act or under section 5 of the Federal Trade Commission Act (1914).

Price Discrimination

Price discrimination is the practice of selling some homogeneous product—a good of "like grade and quality"—to different buyers at different prices. For instance, if a firm sells homogeneous salt to different buyers at different prices, the firm has price discriminated. The price difference is itself the price discrimination, and it can be illegal (except under certain conditions outlined below) when it may substantially lessen competition or tend to create a monopoly.

In antitrust practice, the phrase "may substantially lessen competition" has come to mean that competition is reduced—and the law violated—whenever there is some adverse effect, or probable adverse effect, on other business organizations in the market. In the salt-selling example, the price discrimination may tend to adversely effect some rival salt manufacturer who loses sales and thus profits, or it may tend to injure wholesale buyers who pay the higher prices and are in competition with low-paying buyers. The seller can be found guilty in either instance, and buyers who knowingly receive illegal price discriminations can also be found guilty under the law.

The fundamental difficulty with a law that prohibits price discrimination is that it tends to treat any adverse effect upon rival firms as a reduction in competition that can violate the law. But this treatment of competition is an example of the classic error in anti-

45

trust economics. Price reductions are an essential part of any competitive process, and so is the movement of resources from higher-cost sellers to lower-cost sellers. If consumer-buyers tend to purchase more from low-cost sellers, then it is entirely appropriate that high-cost sellers lose sales or have their business adversely affected. To interfere with this process and to prosecute the firms with the lower prices—and it is only the lower prices that threaten competitors—is blatantly protectionist of the existing market structure of suppliers.

Some might argue that this criticism is too severe because sellers accused of price discrimination can attempt to demonstrate, in their defense, that they have price discriminated in "good faith" in order to meet competition (from some rival seller, presumably) or that the price discrimination can be fully justified by specific cost savings. In practice, however, these so-called absolute defenses have proven unsatisfactory. It is inherently unclear when price reductions are in "good faith," and aggressive competitors often attempt to beat, not meet, prices charged by rivals. Further, the cost-savings defense is all but illusory since it requires a level of technical precision in cost accounting, especially in accounting overhead costs, that may simply be impossible; specific price reductions by multiproduct companies on specific products can rarely be cost justified to the legal satisfaction of the FTC or the courts.[1] Thus, the bulk of the firms indicted for price discrimination—that is, for price competition—have failed to defend themselves successfully; they have lost or abandoned their cases, and then they have raised their prices to comply with the law.

There is now little professional debate over the intent and effect of the price-discrimination law: they have clearly been to reduce price competition and to protect high-cost, high-priced businesses from the resource-reallocation process. Like minimum-wage laws, agricultural price supports, and National Recovery Act codes during the Great Depression, the Robinson-Patman Act was depression legislation aimed at reducing the rigors of the market by restricting price competition.[2] Presumably, the justification claimed for such a

[1] Herbert F. Taggard, Cost Justification (Ann Arbor: School of Business Administration, University of Michigan, 1959).

[2] The Robinson-Patman Act (1936) was reportedly drafted by the U.S. Wholesale Grocers Association. See Richard Caves, American Industry: Structure, Conduct, Performance, 2d ed. (Englewood Cliffs, N.J.: Prentice-Hall, 1967), p. 86.

46

law in the 1930s is no longer relevant, if it ever was. Today the law's only effect is to stifle the competitive market process.

The Borden evaporated milk case is a classic example of the irrationalities associated with attempting to enforce a law against price discrimination. In 1958, the Borden Company was indicted by the Federal Trade Commission for selling evaporated milk of like grade and quality to different buyers at different prices. Borden charged a lower price for milk that it packed and sold to private-label customers than it charged for its own Borden-brand ("Elsie") milk. Since the milk in both instances was chemically the same, the FTC charged that the price differences amounted to price discrimination in violation of the law.[3]

The milk at the factory may well have been the same, but consumer perception of the milk at retail was demonstrably not the same. Consumers were willing to pay more for the Borden brand of evaporated milk than for milk packed by Borden but sold under various private labels. Perhaps consumers were willing to pay more because the Borden Company had established a substantial reputation for high-quality products, which generations of consumers had come to rely on. For example, Borden carefully controlled the shelf life of its own brand of milk, whereas its responsibilities for private-label milk ended when the milk was packed and sold. In addition, some of Borden's expenses, such as advertising, transportation, and labels, did not apply to its private-label milk, and this may have made it possible for Borden to charge lower prices to the private-label distributors. In short, there were both demand and cost differences with respect to the different brands of evaporated milk that could easily have rationalized the general differences in the prices of the products.

Even more important, however, the lower prices Borden charged to private-label distributors involved no injury to any of the parties involved: not to the private-label distributors themselves, who willingly purchased the milk from Borden; not to the customers of the private-label milk, who, presumably, bought a quality milk product at a lower price; and not to Borden's own customers of its "premium" evaporated milk, who could have switched to cheaper milks at any time but did not. There was never any question of monopoly in private-label evaporated-milk production, since Borden never did more than 11 percent of the Midwest private-label packing, a

[3]*In the Matter of the Borden Company*, 381 FTC 130 (1958).

share it had legitimately gained because of the locational advantages of its creameries.

The real issue in the FTC's long harassment of Borden hinged, as it turned out, on the fact that some smaller, independent creameries in the Midwest had lost some private-label business and a few had even gone out of business. There was nothing in the FTC's records to indicate that the Borden Company was involved directly in their demise; indeed, some of these creameries had disappeared prior to Borden's entry into private-label milk packing. And yet it is perfectly clear from the 1966 FTC decision against Borden that the loss of these independent creameries was the tendency to "lessen competition" that had concerned the FTC. The long legal harassment concerned Borden's ability to provide economic advantages to willing customers and the inability—for reasons unrelated to Borden—of some of its rivals to perform in a similar manner. Thus the thrust of the enforcement of the anti–price discrimination law was purely protectionist of an inefficient market structure of firms. The case against Borden was ultimately dismissed in 1967,[4] but the meaning of the case and the decades of FTC enforcement of Robinson-Patman remain clear beyond all doubt: high-cost rivals are to be protected in the name of preserving competition.

The new direction in antitrust policy is, literally, not to actively enforce Robinson-Patman. Only persistent discrimination that would result in "monopoly" would, presumably, now concern the FTC. This is an excellent development in the administration of the antitrust laws, but there is no guarantee that it will be permanent. The case for antitrust repeal is, in fact, at its strongest with respect to the Robinson-Patman Act.[5] A law against price discrimination, which prosecutes successful firms in the name of preserving competition in the "public interest," has no theoretical or empirical support.

Tying Agreements

Tying agreements, such as territorial restrictions, full-line forcing, and tie-in sales, are voluntary contractual agreements between the sellers and buyers of products or services that typically restrict the activities of buyers in certain ways. For example, buyers might sign an agreement to purchase good or service X on condition that they

---

[4]*Borden Company* v. *FTC*, 381 F. 2nd. 175 (1967).

[5]Wesley J. Liebeler, "The Robinson-Patman Act: Let's Repeal It!" *Antitrust Law Journal* 44 (April 1976): 18–43.

also purchase good or service Y from the same seller. Or a territorial restriction in a contract might forbid some distributor of a product from selling the product in the territory of another distributor. Tying agreements on the sale or lease of shoe machines might include a clause restricting service on the machines. A manufacturer might lease a copier on condition that the leasee use the ink or paper supplied by the copier manufacturer or some subsidiary. Finally, a maker of brand-name blue jeans might attempt to restrict sales to certain distributors or to fix the minimum resale price of the jeans through contract.

The older, general consensus was that these restrictive practices could injure competition and final consumers and should be prohibited when any substantial volume of business was involved. The courts, up to 1977, strongly supported this consensus. Recently, however, professional opinion on some restrictive practices has shifted markedly. The newer view holds that it is not immediately obvious why a manufacturer would want to injure its own distributors or the final customers of its own product. Nor is it immediately obvious how purely vertical business restraints could lead to any horizontal output restriction and any higher market price.

It is possible that certain vertical restrictive agreements might only be an attempt to price discriminate, or preserve goodwill, or shift certain business risks, or financially strengthen certain distributors, or curtail inefficient "free riding" activity.[6] A manufacturer of personal computers, for example, might want distributors to provide considerable presale information or postsale service. In the absence of some restrictive agreement, customers might decide to "free ride" off the information provided by full-service distributors and then purchase their equipment from discounters. The resulting intra-brand competition might ultimately force the full-service, authorized dealers to drop the expensive presale information, which could hurt the manufacturer in inter-brand competition. A restrictive agreement between the manufacturer and its distributors that territorially restricts those distributors or protects dealer profit margins through resale price-maintenance agreements could remedy

---

[6]See, for example, the discussion in Richard A. Posner, *Antitrust Law: An Economic Perspective* (Chicago: University of Chicago Press, 1976), pp. 171–84. See also idem, "The Next Step in the Antitrust Treatment of Restricted Distribution: Per Se Legality," *University of Chicago Law Review* 48 (Winter 1981): 6–26.

the situation and allow more efficient rivalry with other computer manufacturers.

The economic rationale for restrictive tying agreements was finally recognized by the Supreme Court in 1977 in the *Sylvania* case.[7] Sylvania, a relatively small manufacturer of television sets, had been sued under the antitrust laws by one of its distributors, Continental, for preventing Continental from establishing a new distributorship in Sacramento, California, where Sylvania had another authorized dealer. Sylvania argued that any additional intra-brand competition would have weakened both the competing dealerships and Sylvania's ability to compete inter-brand with stronger rival manufacturers and distributors, such as Sears and Zenith. Since Sylvania was a relatively small manufacturer attempting to hold on to a declining market share, and not some near-monopolist about to crush all its competition, the Supreme Court accepted this particular dealer restriction as reasonable. And although a rule-of-reason approach to restrictive agreements is not entirely satisfactory (see chapter 4), the repudiation of per se illegality in *Sylvania* was certainly a movement in the right direction, that is, toward per se legality.

Resale Price-Maintenance Agreements

Resale price-maintenance agreements—vertical agreements restricting price—still remain illegal per se, but even here the law may be on the verge of change. The theoretical case for allowing certain restrictive agreements can be extended to vertical price agreements, and even the antitrust authorities now seem prepared to accept a rule of reason in their regard.[8]

Most of the distaste for resale price maintenance goes back to the depression and the years immediately following, when the so-called fair-trade laws existed. The fair-trade laws legalized resale price-maintenance contracts by exempting them from federal antitrust regulation. However, these laws often went well beyond simply permitting restrictive vertical price agreements between willing buyers and sellers. The notorious non-signer clauses provided that any

---

[7]*Continental T.V. Inc.* v. *GTE Sylvania, Inc.*, 433 U.S. 36 (1977).

[8]Terry Calvani and James Langenfeld, "An Overview of the Current Debate on Resale Price Maintenance," *Contemporary Policy Issues* 3 (Spring 1985): 1–8. See also Thomas R. Overstreet, Jr., *Resale Price Maintenance: Economic Theories and Evidence*, Bureau of Economics Staff Report to the Federal Trade Commission (November 1983).

retailer that refused to sign a fair-trade contract with a manufacturer could, nonetheless, be legally bound by the terms of agreements signed by others![9]

Depression policymakers were extremely hostile toward price competition, believing it to be one of the major reasons for the prolonged economic stagnation of the 1930s. Chain-store taxes and nonsigner clauses to limit price reductions were only two examples of that hostility. Needless to say, modern proponents of free trade do not support legally restrictive nonsigner clauses. They hold only that resale price-maintenance agreements should be exempted from the antitrust law. It would then be up to manufacturers and distributors to make such agreements voluntarily, if they so desired; it should not be the function of government to prohibit such contracts or coerce any firm into them.

Vertical Merger Agreements

The ultimate vertical restrictive agreement between a manufacturer and a distributor is a vertical merger. A shoe manufacturer, for example, that purchases a retail shoe distributor could certainly proceed to fix resale prices in its own stores. A vertically integrated manufacturer might order its wholly owned retailer to exclude the shoes of a manufacturing competitor. A shoe manufacturer could purchase a leather supplier and either foreclose leather supplies to a rival or direct that the leather be sold at a higher price, in order to squeeze the rival between high input costs and low shoe prices at retail.

The arguments that such activities provide a rationale for antitrust policy is weak and unconvincing. The competitive market process cannot be injured by any of them. Rival shoe manufacturers, excluded from some retail outlets, would not be excluded from the shoe market; presumably there are other retail outlets, and more could always be created. Higher prices for leather in an openly competitive leather market would only mean lower leather sales and lower profits. And the selling of less leather—or fewer shoes—can in no way be ultimately profitable to the larger, vertically integrated company.

There is, of course, one development that may tend to exclude rival sellers: successful vertical integration that results in improved

---

[9]The non-signers clause was declared constitutional, in Illinois, by the Supreme Court in *Old Dearborn Distribution Co.* v. *Seagram Distillers, Corp.*, 299 U.S. 183 (1936).

efficiency and lower costs and prices. Indeed, the only mergers or integrations that ever threaten rivals are mergers in which the merged firms benefit from integration economies and intend to pass along some of the benefits to consumers in the form of lower prices or improved services. Such mergers might well induce nonintegrated firms to plan similar cost-saving integrations, and, from a consumer perspective, the sooner such integrations occur, the better. To prohibit these mergers, in the so-called public interest, would be the height of economic irrationality.

The *Brown Shoe* case of 1962 nicely capsulizes all that is wrong with legal regulation of vertical integration.[10] Brown Shoe, a manufacturer of shoes, bought the Kinney chain of retail shoe stores in 1956. By the court's own admission, the merger would have allowed Brown to realize certain economies and efficiencies, such as faster style changes and lower shoe prices, which it might have been able to pass along to shoe customers. Such a development would have put competitive pressure on nonintegrated shoe manufacturers and retailers and encouraged them to vertically integrate, too. But this trend toward concentration—already evident in the shoe industry, according to the court—was allegedly destructive of competition and certainly contrary to the congressional intention. Thus, despite its obvious consumer benefits, the merger was declared illegal and Brown was ordered to divest itself of Kinney.

From the standpoint of consumer welfare, there was absolutely no reason for the judgment against Brown Shoe. Brown was a relatively small manufacturer of shoes in 1956, with 4 percent of domestic output, and Kinney owned only 845 retail outlets out of an industry total of more than 70,000. The shoe manufacturing and shoe retailing markets were easy for new firms to enter. Concentration in the shoe industry was not increasing, despite the court's insinuations to the contrary. And finally, the court's treatment of business efficiency as an exclusionary restraint of trade stands antitrust precisely on its head. If *Brown Shoe* was not the worst decision in antitrust history (there is, after all, a lot of competition!),[11] it certainly takes a high rank.

---

[10]*United States* v. *Brown Shoe Company*, 370 U.S. 294 (1962).

[11]Ward Bowman nominates *Utah Pie Company* v. *Continental Baking Company*, 386 U.S. 685 (1967). See Ward Bowman, "Restraint of Trade by the Supreme Court: The Utah Pie Case," *Yale Law Journal* 77 (November 1967): 70–85.

Conclusions

Antitrust has come a long way since *Borden* and *Brown Shoe*. The dominant opinion today is that price discrimination and vertical agreements do not generally present any serious threat to consumer welfare and that such activity ought not to be legally restrained because of some adverse effect on rival sellers. Antitrust critics agree, of course, but some would go further to abolish the Clayton Act altogether, to be sure that such abominations as *Borden* and *Brown Shoe* never occur again.

V. Horizontal Agreements: Merger and Price Fixing

The last remaining stronghold of strict antitrust enforcement is the continuing regulation of horizontal agreements, such as joint ventures, price agreements, and horizontal mergers, that have the probability of reducing market output and raising market prices. The general antitrust thinking on horizontal agreements is that most mergers and joint agreements should be judged by an economic rule of reason, while price collusion and division-of-market agreements should remain illegal per se.

The rule-of-reason approach implies that the antitrust authorities evaluate and act upon the probable social costs and benefits of a proposed merger or joint venture. Joint business agreements can promise substantial cost savings in production and distribution, as well as in financing, industrial research, and product development. In addition, they may allow the innovation of entirely new products and services not feasible without inter-firm cooperation. On the other hand, there is always the possibility that mergers and joint ventures may lead to output restriction and the suppression of price rivalry. The antitrust authorities and the courts, therefore, must weigh the probabilities of increased social benefits against the risks and costs of potential output restriction. Under a rule of reason, mergers whose probable benefits exceed the probable costs would be allowed, and those whose probable costs exceed the probable benefits would be prohibited.

The rule-of-reason approach is not yet generally accepted for dealing with price-fixing or division-of-market agreements; the consensus is that they should still remain illegal per se.[1] Since it is widely assumed that the social benefits associated with price fixing are minuscule or altogether nonexistent, and since such agreements

---

[1]Robert H. Bork, *The Antitrust Paradox: A Policy at War with Itself* (New York: Basic Books, 1978), chap. 13. See also the classic article by idem, "The Rule of Reason and the Per Se Concept: Price Fixing and Market Division," *Yale Law Journal* 75 (January 1966): 375–475.

intend to restrict market output, they can be safely excluded from any rule-of-reason analysis and prohibited entirely. Finally, it is hoped that the legal certainty of the per se approach to price fixing will have a chilling effect on this activity in the future.

Although a rule-of-reason approach to mergers and joint ventures sounds appropriate, and although a flat prohibition on price and output restrictions—so-called naked agreements—also sounds appropriate, these positions are fraught with many significant difficulties. The essential problem is that both approaches assume that the antitrust authorities or the courts can have access to information concerning the future course of the market process that is simply unavailable to any regulatory authority or court. In addition, both approaches assume an ability to measure economic phenomena that, in principle, cannot be measured by any outside observer. Thus, while both approaches may give the appearance of science and objectivity, both are, in fact, pseudoscientific and cannot legitimize government antitrust intervention in this area.

The Rule of Reason: Social Costs

The rule-of-reason approach implies that the antitrust authorities ought to permit horizontal agreements when the social gains are expected to exceed the social losses. Social losses relate to the probability that the agreement could reduce market output, and that probability depends, in turn, upon whether the agreement creates any so-called market power or not. According to conventional theory, market power depends directly on the market share of the firms involved and whether the increase in market concentration makes effective output restriction more probable.

The Antitrust Division of the Justice Department and the Federal Trade Commission have published new horizontal merger guidelines (revised from 1968) that are based on the Herfindahl Index of market concentration.[2] A business merger that raises the Herfindahl Index by more than a stated number of points or pushes the industry index above a stated level will probably trigger legal action by the government in opposition to the merger. As noted in chapter 1, the

---

[2]For an explanation of the Herfindahl Index, see David S. Weinstock, "Using the Herfindahl Index to Measure Concentration," *Antitrust Bulletin* 27 (Summer 1982): 285–97. For a critical analysis of the 1982 merger guidelines, see Frank Easterbrook, "An Economic Analysis of the 1982 Justice Department Guidelines for Horizontal Mergers," *Minnesota Law Review* 67 (April 1983): 749–92.

guidelines have been employed to restrain mergers in the beer and steel industries.

Merger guidelines rest on two crucial assumptions. The first is the notion that there is some scientific way to define the so-called relevant market under discussion in any merger. The second is the belief that there is some scientific way to determine precisely which levels of market concentration generate market power and which do not. In fact, the relevant market can never be known with scientific accuracy. Further, it is impossible—theoretically and empirically—to know which levels of market concentration generate market power.

Relevant Market

A rational discussion of market concentration is premised on some acceptable definition of "relevant market." Firms are said to compete in some relevant market, and presumably a merger or joint venture may threaten to create, or to increase, market power. If relevant markets are defined narrowly, almost any horizontal agreement will increase market concentration and threaten to create market power. If, on the other hand, relevant markets are defined very broadly (and the merging firms usually hope they are), there is almost no horizontal agreement that could threaten to create market power. The question, then, is how to define relevant markets in order to calculate the appropriate levels of market concentration.

In general, a relevant market includes all suppliers whose products are "reasonable substitutes" for each other and excludes all others. If one were evaluating a possible merger between two soft-drink companies, for example, or between a soft-drink company and a beer company, one would have to determine whether the products produced and sold by the different companies were reasonable substitutes for each other. Narrowly, one could consider products to be substitutes (and their suppliers to be competitors) when a price adjustment by one supplier directly affects the output and sales of another. For instance, if soft-drink price changes directly affect beer sales, then, presumably, soft drinks and beer are reasonable substitutes and the relevant market in any possible merger would have to include at least both these products and suppliers.

But there are important difficulties with this approach. In the first place, it may be impossible to determine, in practice, whether changes in the prices of soft drinks caused the change in beer sales. Second,

57

changes in the prices of a soft drink—other prices remaining the same—may not be significant enough to affect beer sales appreciably; nonprice elements of rivalry may be important, even more important than price. The fact that beer sales are not appreciably affected by some soft-drink price change does not necessarily mean that soft-drink and beer firms are not rivals. It may imply only that price changes are a poor measure of substitutability in markets where nonprice competition is important.

What, precisely, is the relevant market for soft drinks? Is it only soft drinks, or does it also include fruit drinks, orange juice, milk, bottled water, wine, and beer? Does it include only U.S. manufacturers and sellers, or are producers in Canada and Holland to be included? Should the relevant market be defined nationally, or should it be divided into regional submarkets? How are these questions to be answered unambiguously?

These are not rhetorical questions. In traditional merger discussions, the definition of the precise relevant market can make all the difference. If the relevant market for soft drinks is restricted to soft drinks, then almost any merger between big soft-drink companies can look potentially output threatening. If the market for soft drinks extends beyond soft drinks, however, many more horizontal agreements can be permitted. In the absence of an unambiguous definition of the relevant market, it would seem impossible to determine with scientific certainty whether changes in market share or in levels of concentration threaten competition and make effective output restriction more probable.

Market Share and Market Power

Even if relevant markets could be clearly defined, there is an additional threshold problem associated with any rule of reason. Government merger guidelines may be useful in indicating to business the likelihood of antitrust action, but they are of no scientific value in theoretical discussions of market power, and they cannot justify government intervention. Although the general public has the impression that there must be some good reason for the antitrust authorities' choice of particular limits in the Herfindahl Index of market concentration, those limits are completely arbitrary. No one—and certainly not the antitrust authorities—can ever know whether a merger of firms that creates, say, a 36 percent market share—or one that raises the Herfindahl Index by 150 points—can create sufficient economic power to reduce market output and raise market price. No one knows, or can know, whether monopoly power begins at a 36 percent market share or a 36.74 percent market share. Neither economic theory nor empirical evidence can justify any merger guideline or prohibition.[3]

Even if relevant-market and market-concentration considerations were not ambiguous and arbitrary, there would still not be sufficient reason to legally restrict horizontal agreements. All the issues confronted in chapter 2 concerning the ability of firms in free markets to actually charge long-run monopoly prices and earn monopoly profits are relevant here and need not be repeated. It is enough to point out that antitrust theory cannot demonstrate that firms in free markets can earn long-run monopoly prices and profits or that resources in free markets can be inefficiently misallocated. By definition, a free market is always competitive and tends to eliminate inefficiency.

Output Restriction

Yet a further problem in applying a rule of reason to horizontal mergers and joint agreements is the difficulty of measuring output restriction and determining that it is the result of monopoly power. Existing production cannot be compared against the standard of pure competition (see chapter 2); nor can the premerger industry output level be considered the appropriate level of production. The premerger output level is a disequilibrium output level, established through interdependent pricing and output determinations rather than through independent pricing, as under atomistic competition. It cannot serve as a welfare benchmark because there is no difference, in principle, between market-price and output determination in the premerger and postmerger situations. Interdependent pricing and output determination exist under both circumstances, and both are part of an open-market discovery and adjustment process. It is true that legal monopoly could establish an unambiguous output restriction benchmark by prohibiting market entry. But in the absence of some legal restriction on production and market entry, it is impossible to determine whether free-market outputs have been inefficiently restricted. Thus, even a merger resulting in monopoly could not be unambiguously condemned.

[3]Paul A. Pautler, "A Review of the Economic Basis for Broad-Based Horizontal-Merger Policy," *Antitrust Bulletin* 28 (Fall 1983): 571–651.

The Rule of Reason: Social Benefits

The social-benefit side of the rule-of-reason equation poses as many difficulties as the social-cost side. Generally, the social benefits associated with horizontal agreements include economies and efficiencies of inter-firm production, financing, advertising, distribution, marketing, and research and development. Some of these benefits are measurable and objective; some are subtle and subjective. Some require financial and accounting skills to understand; others are anticipations and expectations based upon entrepreneurial experience in these matters. The question is whether the antitrust authorities or the courts can evaluate the probable benefits of horizontal agreement as accurately as the relevant entrepreneurs, or, even more fundamentally, whether parties outside an agreement can correctly evaluate future benefits at all.

Businessmen and entrepreneurs, standing in for owners, have strong incentives to estimate inter-firm benefits and costs correctly; their own success and even the very life of their corporations may well be at stake. One would assume, therefore, that businessmen considering horizontal agreements would be especially careful to obtain the most accurate information available concerning the possible financial effects of any merger or joint venture.

It is important to note, however, the inherently subjective element in all entrepreneurial calculation concerning future costs and benefits. Successful businessmen can discover and exploit profit opportunities that are not obvious and that others do not "see," and this entrepreneurial process goes well beyond simple cost accounting and economic calculation.[4] Successful business agreements appear to be like successful marriages; they work efficiently, but only the parties involved can understand the relative costs and benefits. Moreover, like marriages, their continued success depends more on tacit knowledge and understanding than on any objective cost-benefit calculations.

The only objective ex post test of the correctness of entrepreneurial decisions is the market process itself. If the businessmen who enter into a horizontal agreement are correct concerning probable

---

[4]See, for example, Israel Kirzner, *Discovery and the Capitalist Process* (Chicago: University of Chicago Press, 1985), pp. 15–39. Even Robert Bork has admitted that the efficiencies associated with agreement are impossible to measure quantitatively and that the most important ones may be "intangible and develop gradually over time." See Bork, "Rule of Reason," p. 386.

costs and benefits, then the merged firm's market performance will likely be enhanced and its market share and profits may well increase. On the other hand, if the entrepreneurs have miscalculated, then the organization will likely waste economic resources and lose market share to relatively more efficient rivals and competitors. In either case, there is no legitimate reason to believe that the antitrust authorities or courts can have direct knowledge of these costs and benefits or that their intervention can be a reasonable substitute for a working out of a market process.

The Per Se Approach

The logic for an absolute prohibition of horizontal price collusion is that such collusion intends output restriction—a social cost—but creates little, if any, opportunity for the generation of social benefits because they do not involve an integration of facilities between firms. Economic analysis and so-called considerations of law-enforcement efficiency dictate that they remain illegal per se.

But the difficulties of evaluating mergers with a rule of reason are also encountered when trying to bring a per se perspective to bear on price-fixing agreements. One can argue, first, that efficiencies and cost savings to society may indeed be associated with such agreements. Second, although such agreements may intend to restrict production and increase group profits, they are generally not able to do so.

Price Coordination and Efficiency

Over the last few years several commentators have argued that the reduction in risk associated with horizontal price coordination in open and uncertain markets could increase market output and enhance consumer welfare;[5] it may also lead to information-cost and price adjustment-cost savings.[6] Indeed, respected antitrust scholar Frank Easterbrook now considers a rule-of-reason approach toward all horizontal price agreements to be justified.[7]

---

[5]See, for example, S. Y. Wu, "An Essay on Monopoly Power and Stable Price Policy," *American Economic Review* 69 (March 1979): 60–72.

[6]Donald Dewey, "Information, Entry and Welfare: The Case for Collusion," *American Economic Review* 69 (September 1979): 587–94. See also H. B. Malmgren, "Information, Expectations, and the Theory of the Firm," *Quarterly Journal of Economics* 75 (August 1961): 399–421.

[7]Frank Easterbrook, "Fixing the Price Fixing Confusion: A Rule of Reason Approach," *Yale Law Journal* 92 (March 1983): 706–30.

A number of efficiencies are possible from price and output coordination among firms operating under conditions of market uncertainty and imperfect information—the normal conditions. Price adjustments can be costly to both buyers and sellers; price coordination could limit price changes and reduce price-adjustment costs. Price information can in some markets be costly to obtain; price coordination could lower information costs. Price uncertainty for risk-averse buyers could reduce their purchases, and price uncertainty for risk-averse sellers could reduce their market output; price coordination could reduce risk and increase sales and market output. Price coordination could stabilize output and inventory fluctuations in the short run and lead to greater market outputs and lower costs in the long run. The uncertainties of market entry could be reduced, and entry encouraged, if potential entrants could make price and output agreements. Price uncertainty could restrict nonprice rivalry; price coordination could lead to additional research and innovation.

Support for a per se illegality approach to price-fixing schemes presumes that it is possible to know beforehand which business combinations will generate net social efficiency and which will not. This presumes that the very information provided by the working out of the market process can be known before that market process is allowed to operate. The point here is not that cartels and market-division agreements are always appropriate or that they always increase social welfare. But, absent an open market process, there is no scientific way to conclude that such arrangements are always socially inappropriate or should be illegal per se.

The knowledge problem and the discovery principle with respect to price coordination are exemplified in the needless controversy over the expiration of the Reed-Bulwinkle Act (1948), which had generally exempted the trucking industry from Sherman Act jurisdiction. The industry maintains that it requires a partial continuation of that exemption so that industry rate-bureau organizations can legally continue to coordinate routes and prices for member truckers.[8] Antitrust enthusiasts maintain, on the other hand, that collective rate making constitutes horizontal price collusion, a judgment that would continue to frustrate the welfare advantages asso-

---

[8]See, for example, Jerry A. Hausman, "Information Costs, Competition, and Collective Rate Making in the Motor Carrier Industry," paper prepared for the Motor Carrier Ratemaking Study Commission, August 16, 1982.

ciated with deregulation and increasing competition in the trucking industry.[9]

Clearly, the only way to discover whether collective rate making, on balance, serves shippers or not is to permit the activity to continue in a free and unregulated transportation market. Industry rate bureaus have performed a price- and route-coordination function in trucking for many decades, and it is unclear, under conditions of free entry, why that activity should now be legally restricted or prohibited. If certain carriers employ rate-bureau services and achieve efficiencies, then those carriers may gain business and market-share relative to other carriers that price and route independently. If, on the other hand, the costs to shippers exceed the value provided by price coordination, the carriers may lose business and market-share to carriers that price independently. In either case, there is no ex ante logic for a per se prohibition.

Furthermore, there is no logic for replacing Interstate Commerce Commission regulation in transportation with regulation by the Antitrust Division of the Justice Department. ICC rate regulation, route control, and entry restrictions have stood in the way of a truly competitive open market process in trucking for 50 years, and the industry is now being deregulated in order to discover how it should be organized for efficient service to customers. At this point antitrust enthusiasts are arguing that it is necessary, again, for the government to determine—this time through antitrust regulation—whether industry rate bureaus are socially appropriate or not.

Antitrust advocates contend that rate bureaus in trucking are socially "inefficient," just as the ICC argued for decades that open market competition in trucking would be "destructive." But it should be apparent that neither regulators nor economists—nor attorneys, nor judges—can know what is socially efficient and what is not. That is precisely the purpose of open markets. If industry rate bureaus, on balance, are inefficient, then they will become ineffective and they will dissolve. If they are not inefficient, they will continue to function. But these are questions that can be answered

[9]For an interesting discussion of these issues, see Paul R. Duke, "The Impact of the Removal of Antitrust Immunity on Collective Ratemaking in the Motor Carrier Industry," statement before the Motor Carrier Ratemaking Study Commission, Boston, March 19, 1982. See also Andrew Popper, "The Antitrust System: An Impediment to the Development of Negotiation Models," *American University Law Review* 32 (Winter 1983): 283–334.

only in a deregulated transportation market with total antitrust immunity for carriers.

Those who support the per se illegality of price agreements argue that whatever social advantages might result from those agreements can be achieved more readily and more acceptably through direct contract integration. If firms are really serious about achieving coordination efficiencies, they can always merge or enter formal joint-venture agreements. But why, one might ask in response, should all business coordination be forced to take the path of formal integration? Contract integration may well provide additional, and significant, economies, but surely the firms involved—not the Antitrust Division—can determine whether additional economies do exist, given the risks associated with formal integration. If contract integration can easily lead to additional net-efficiency gains, firms will be only too anxious to pursue it. On the other hand, the advantages of price coordination may well represent all the net gains expected from inter-firm agreement. In that case, loose price coordination is socially efficient.

In an uncertain world, loose price coordination may be a far more flexible device for achieving possible economies than formal contract integration. The risks and costs of formal integration under conditions of uncertainty may be considerable, and loose associations that allow firms to be rivalrous at any moment may well represent a near-optimal social organization. To mandate that firms be completely rivalrous at every moment may cost the economy the efficiencies associated with inter-firm coordination. Yet, to press firms anxious to coordinate some activities into formal integration agreements and their attendant risks may make just as little sense from an efficiency perspective. The appropriate solution is to permit the firms themselves to select the degree of coordination appropriate to the problem to be solved. Again, no antitrust regulation is warranted.

Price Agreements and Output Restriction

The other major argument against the per se illegality of price-fixing agreements, which is especially relevant if social efficiencies are indeed associated with them, is that there is little reason to expect such agreements to be harmful to society. Market-division agreements are, in the absence of direct government support, tenuous at best and tend to break apart in open markets when they are inappropriate. Genuine output-restricting agreements appear generally to be short lived and unable to withstand changing market conditions. When markets are legally open to entry and rivalry, market conditions will normally neutralize attempts to simply reduce market output and raise market prices.

The public can easily be misled on the effectiveness of price conspiracy, often accepting conviction in price-fixing antitrust cases as evidence of effective output restriction and higher prices. This inference, is not, however, normally warranted. Under the law, price agreements themselves are illegal per se; merely to have made an agreement—whether it works or not—is sufficient to violate the antitrust statutes. Whether market outputs were actually restricted or prices were higher during the conspiracy is usually immaterial in government price-conspiracy cases. Indeed, firms indicted for price fixing under the Sherman Antitrust Act often enter *nolo contendere* pleas because they recognize that the existence of an agreement, notwithstanding its effectiveness, is sufficient for conviction.

The classic *Addyston* case illustrates some of the traditional difficulties associated with the per se approach to price-fixing agreements.[10] *Addyston* concerned a conspiracy of six cast-iron-pipe companies that attempted to rig the bid prices for pipe sold to water departments in municipal governments in the 1890s. The precedent set in *Addyston* is one of the most important in all antitrust law. Circuit Judge Taft, in his review of the *Addyston* case on appeal from the district court, argued that the bid-price agreements were illegal in and of themselves; they appeared to intend only a suppression of competition among the firms, to their mutual advantage. Hence, no economic analysis—rule of reason—of the prices actually charged was necessary to condemn the arrangement.[11] Justice Peckham, writing for a unanimous Supreme Court in 1899, agreed with Taft's analysis and decision, as have many important antitrust scholars. Robert Bork, for instance, once called Taft's decision "one of the greatest, if not the greatest, antitrust opinions in the history of the law."[12]

Recent analysis of *Addyston*, however, raises serious questions about such evaluations. After all, the per se approach purposely obscures the very economic issues that may be relevant in such cases. In *Addyston*, for example, Judge Taft, and later Bork, assumed

---

[10]*Addyston Pipe and Steel Company et al. v. United States,* 175 U.S. 211 (1899).

[11]*United States* v. *Addyston Pipe and Steel Company et al.,* 84 F. Supp. 293 (1897).

[12]Bork, *The Antitrust Paradox,* p. 26.

65

that there were no important economic efficiencies associated with the price agreement and that the conspiracy restricted market production and raised the market price for cast-iron pipe—assumptions that may well have been false.

George Bittlingmayer's detailed account of the *Addyston* case makes it clear that some "cooperative solution to market allocation" was necessary to achieve reasonably efficient cast-iron pipe production in this industry in the late 1890s. There was simply no "competitive" equilibrium in the pipe market, he argues, that was consistent with industry cost and demand conditions. With a very cyclical and unstable market demand for pipe, and with decreasing long-run average and marginal costs associated with producing pipe, "competitive" (marginal cost) pricing would not have allowed the various firms to fully recover their costs. Market prices would have been perpetually below average cost, and most of the firms would have eventually become insolvent. Thus, he reasons, some degree of inter-firm cooperation—the bid-rigging scheme, for example—was required to keep plants operating efficiently and to maintain capacity during slack periods of demand.[13]

The available evidence also suggests that pipe prices, even with extensive collusion, were not generally sustained above marginal costs—let alone average costs. Inevitable rivalry within the conspiracy and from firms with significant pipe-production capacity not party to the conspiracy, as well as wide and unanticipated fluctuations in the demand for pipe, made effective long-run price conspiracy impossible.[14] The presumption, therefore, that these agreements allowed the recovery of monopoly prices and monopoly profits with no off-setting social benefits appears totally unwarranted. Such presumptions are probably unwarranted in several other classic price-fixing conspiracies as well.[15]

[13]George Bittlingmayer, "Decreasing Average Cost and Competition: A New Look at the Addyston Pipe Case," *Journal of Law and Economics* 25 (October 1982): 201–29; idem, "Price-Fixing and the Addyston Pipe Case," *Research in Law and Economics* 5 (1983): 57–130. When this simple price agreement was declared illegal per se by the Court in 1899, the conspirators in *Addyston* formally merged to form a corporation called U.S. Cast Iron Pipe and Foundry.

[14]This conclusion may have been initially suggested in Almarin Phillips, *Market Structure, Organization and Performance* (Cambridge: Harvard University Press, 1962).

[15]See, for example, the discussion of the electrical-equipment conspiracy and other noted price-fixing cases in D. T. Armentano, *Antitrust and Monopoly: Anatomy of a Policy Failure* (New York: John Wiley and Sons, 1982), chap. 5.

Conclusions

Criticism of the per se approach to large mergers and horizontal agreements should not be misinterpreted as support for a rule of reason. Although any rule of reason would be an improvement over per se illegality, the rule-of-reason approach itself is fatally flawed. No antitrust policy can be scientifically rationalized for mergers and other horizontal business agreements; the law should neither help nor hinder them.

VI. Liberty, Efficiency, and Antitrust Policy

The argument against antitrust policy presented here has, to this point, been entirely economic. There are, however, some noneconomic considerations that must be brought to bear on an analysis of antitrust regulation. Antitrust laws stand in direct violation of civil liberties, individual rights, and due process of law, and these considerations have important implications for the economic, or efficiency, arguments of traditional theories of antitrust. Seen in this perspective, liberty need not be sacrificed to promote economic efficiency; indeed, only the full protection of all property rights can be socially efficient.

Liberty

The administration and enforcement of the antitrust laws have always posed very serious difficulties for those committed to strict notions of individual rights, consent exchange, and due process.[1] The antitrust laws, by their very nature, appear to interfere with private property rights.[2] Antitrust prohibition of price discrimination, merging, price fixing, and even free-market monopolization prevents freely contracting parties who hold legitimate rights to property from making, or refusing to make, certain contractual arrangements that they believe to be in their best interests. Some economists still argue that there is sufficient reason to prohibit such arrangements from some efficiency perspective, although, as has been argued here, the economic case for any antitrust regulation is weak. Economic considerations aside, however, such private activities as price discrimination, merging, tying, and price fixing appear to violate no property rights in the ordinary sense of the term; that

[1]Some of the following discussion is taken, with permission, from D. T. Armentano, "Efficiency, Liberty, and Antitrust Policy," *Cato Journal* 4, no. 3 (Winter 1985): 925–32.

[2]Roger Pilon, "Corporations and Rights: On Treating Corporate People Justly," *Georgia Law Review* 13 (Summer 1979): 1245–1370.

is, they do not necessarily involve force, fraud, or misrepresentation. But from a strictly natural-rights perspective, the antitrust laws *are* inherently violative of property rights. As noted earlier, even Adam Smith, despite his reservations concerning price conspiracy, rejected any antitrust law on the grounds that its execution could not be made "consistent with liberty and justice."

It might be argued that business people and corporations forgo their right to liberty when they collude and restrict production, since such behavior violates the rights of potential buyers. But this understanding of rights is misguided. Producers own their property, or are the trustees of property for owners, and possess all the rights to it, including the absolute right not to use it at all. Similarly, consumers own the rights to their own property, including the absolute right to spend or not spend their money. The individual rights—property rights—of neither party can be violated by a refusal to deal or by a partial refusal to deal through a voluntary restraint of trade.

A consumer boycott of a manufacturer's product, for example, does not violate the property rights of the manufacturer; the manufacturer has no right to the consumer's income in the first place. Likewise, a restriction of production on the part of a manufacturer— a producer boycott—cannot violate the rights of consumers, since consumers, absent any contractual arrangement, have no property rights to the manufacturer's product. Thus such restrictive agreements as price fixing—though unpopular—are not invasive of anyone's rights, and government restriction of these voluntary arrangements is, from a rights perspective, unjustified.

An important part of the case against antitrust law and enforcement is normative, relating to basic questions of due process, rights, and justice. Prior to antitrust action and an alleged violation of the law, no one can know what it means to "reduce competition substantially" or to effect "unreasonable" restraints of trade; no one can know with reasonable certainty what a given relevant market is or whether prices were reduced in "good faith." Firms that innovate new products or lower prices may discover, after the fact, that such practices injure competitors, lessen competition, and violate the law. But because the antitrust "law" cannot be known beforehand with any degree of clarity, antitrust law and enforcement are capricious and arbitrary, and those firms and individuals tried under antitrust law can hardly be said to have experienced any real due process of law.[3]

Efficiency

Although economists are often reluctant to discuss normative questions of liberty and rights per se, they do admit for the antitrust area that some freedom, say, the freedom to collude, must be sacrificed (traded off) in order to preserve "competition" and an efficient allocation of resources. Although free markets and carefully defined property rights are held to generally promote economic efficiency, maximizing wealth and minimizing cost, there are alleged to be important exceptions, such as price collusion, in which output can be restrained and prices increased to consumers. *Liberty* must therefore be sacrificed for *efficiency*.

Some theoretical and empirical arguments against this position have already been raised. Here, however, it will be argued that the standard neoclassical theory of efficiency and welfare is untenable and that individual liberty and the complete protection of all property rights can, in fact, be reconciled with economic efficiency properly understood.

Subjective Cost and Benefit

The conventional theory of social efficiency in antitrust depends upon the measurability, at least in principle, of consumer and producer surpluses. The gains and losses associated with restrictive practices are to be weighed, and, since efficiency considerations are relevant, business practices that result in a net increase in social welfare are to be permitted.[4] Other practices, price fixing, for example, are said to create a dead-weight welfare loss and should not be permitted. The problem with this determination is that it cannot actually be made; because individual costs and benefits are ultimately subjective and personal, they cannot be added up or subtracted to calculate net social efficiency or welfare. As I have stated elsewhere:

[3]This treatment has been most obvious in Federal Trade Commission enforcement of the Robinson-Patman Act. See D. T. Armentano, *Antitrust and Monopoly: Anatomy of a Policy Failure* (New York: John Wiley and Sons, 1982), chap. 6.

[4]See, for example, a concise review of the standard economic-welfare model in Wesley J. Liebeler, "Intrabrand Cartels under GTE Sylvania," *UCLA Law Review* 30 (October 1982): 13–17.

The costs of an action are the subjective opportunities forgone by the person who makes the decision; the benefits are the subjective satisfactions. . . . Since costs and benefits are subjective they are not cardinally measurable. There is no standard unit of value that would allow the summing up of individual costs and benefits into social aggregates for comparison. Thus it is misleading to suggest that a rational antitrust policy can weigh the costs against the gains of restrictive agreements, and then decide which agreements are socially efficient and which are not.[5]

A metaphor might illustrate the difficulties of aggregating personal costs and benefits. Assume a temperature of 70 degrees in a room. It is apparent that different people in that room can feel either warm or cold; the 70-degree figure does not actually measure how cold or warm individuals feel but only the level of mercury on an objective scale. The subjective states of warm and cold are not themselves directly knowable or measurable by others, and they are not susceptible to addition, subtraction, comparison, aggregation, or any other mathematical manipulation. Temperature readings can be averaged, but feelings of comfort or discomfort on the part of different individuals cannot be manipulated mathematically.

A perspective on social efficiency well within the neoclassical paradigm is the argument that *all* business agreements ex ante lower costs and that, since opportunity costs are ultimately subjective and personal, such savings can always offset any so-called welfare losses due, say, to higher prices. The easy assumptions in antitrust have always been that the costs associated with certain horizontal agreements greatly outweigh the benefits, if any, and therefore that their regulation or prohibition is justified. Yet if costs are inherently subjective, there is no way cost-benefit judgments can ever be certain.[6] Market-division agreements may end costly crosshauling and advertising. Agreements between competitors in transportation may reduce information and transaction costs. Horizontal agreements that reduce risk and uncertainty can promote efficiency. And since only the parties to an agreement can know the costs and

---

[5]D. T. Armentano, "Antitrust Policy: Reform or Repeal?" Cato Institute Policy Analysis no. 21 (January 18, 1983), pp. 9–10.

[6]Even Robert Bork admits that this position can be intelligently argued. See Robert H. Bork, "The Rule of Reason and the Per Se Concept," *Yale Law Journal* 75 (January 1966): 390.

benefits associated with it, no antitrust regulation of horizontal agreements can be entirely rationalized.

Plan Coordination and Efficiency

Another even bolder perspective on efficiency is plan coordination, which holds that all voluntary agreements, including so-called restrictive agreements, promote efficiency since all aim, ex ante, to bring into coordination the respective plans of various market participants. Since market information is neither perfect nor constant, this process of coordinating plans through agreement can never attain a final equilibrium. But, as already argued, an end-state equilibrium cannot be the focus of any analysis of efficiency. The open market process is the focus of analysis, and it continuously creates powerful incentives to discover and utilize the best information available in order to coordinate plans and correct those that fall short of objectives. Thus, an efficient market is an open and learning market, one that tends to provide the widest scope and encouragement for private plan making, private plan correction, and private plan coordination.

This approach to market efficiency allows an unambiguous condemnation of legal restrictions on competition, cooperation, and entry as being socially harmful—inefficient—since they directly restrict market information and the scope of voluntary plan coordination.[7]

A plan-coordination theory of market efficiency can easily encompass cooperative agreements among businesses, agreements that have always been suspect for, according to conventional analysis, restricting competition and market output. In a plan-coordination theory, rivalry and cooperation are neither antagonists nor opposites but simply different elements in an entrepreneurial process of discovery and adjustment. Presumably, firms continually attempt to improve their own position either as rivals or as participants in joint ventures. Since no outside party can be in a position to directly observe costs and benefits, and since all voluntary agreements can promote efficiency, the determination to be rivalrous or cooperative must be left entirely to the participants in these agreements. Plan-coordination theory undercuts the presumption that the FTC or any regulatory authority or court can rationally determine the social

[7]Gerald P. O'Driscoll, Jr., and Mario J. Rizzo, *The Economics of Time and Ignorance* (Oxford: Basil Blackwell, 1985), pp. 154–58.

efficiency of mergers and joint ventures. It also undercuts the presumption that antitrust regulation can have *any* genuine scientific justification.

Conclusions

Adam Smith was convinced that the system of natural liberty—the free market—would promote the public's economic interest and that government regulation tended to hinder the workings of the competitive market process. He was particularly concerned that legal monopoly—at the behest of specific manufacturing interests—would be employed to restrict free entry into markets and raise prices to consumers. He was aware that businessmen themselves often met to conspire to raise prices; yet he was reluctant to endorse laws to prevent it because they would not be compatible with liberty.

Was Smith's view naive? On the contrary, after almost 100 years of antitrust laws, Smith's insights on monopoly appear particularly incisive. While the antitrust laws are ostensibly intended to promote competition, they have been employed repeatedly—by both government and private plaintiffs—to restrain and restrict the competitive market process. The laws have been used to protect the existing industrial structure, which is exactly what Smith feared most about government monopoly generally. They have served to restrain trade and competition, while the real monopolists in the American business system—the firms that hold legal monopoly—remain relatively immune from antitrust prosecution. Finally, antitrust laws have clearly been abusive of "liberty and justice," exactly as Smith had predicted.

The economic and normative case for the abolition of antitrust law is impressive. The law appears to have lost all of its claim to legitimacy. The burden of proof is now on those who would retain or reform antitrust law, to demonstrate why all the laws should not be repealed.

Index

Justice, U.S. Department of, 1, 12, 56

Kellogg Company, 34
Kirzner, Israel, 33n, 60n
Koller, Ronald H., 43n

Langenfeld, James, 50n
Lavoie, Don, 15n
Liebeler, Wesley J., 48n, 71n
Littlechild, S. C., 27n
Local Government Antitrust Act of 1984, 29n
LTV Corporation, 6

MacAvoy, Paul W., 15n
McGee, John S., 43
McGowan, John J., 3n
McKie, James W., 3n
McNulty, Paul J., 19n
Malmgren, H. B., 61n
Mancke, Richard B., 3n
Mann, H. Michael, 4n, 37n
Mansfield, Edwin, 20n
Mergers
  competitive process and, 5–6
  cost-benefit information re, 12–13
  federal guidelines for, 12, 56–57
  horizontal, 1, 55, 56–61
  inter-firm benefits, determination of, 60–61
  laws re, 45
  legal reforms re, viii
  market-share and -power concerns, 58–59
  output restrictions and, 59
  property rights and, 69–70
  Reagan administration position re, viii
  relevant-market concerns, 57–58
  vertical, 51–52
Miller, James, 7n
Misallocation of resources, 17–18, 22–23
Monopolies
  as barrier to entry, 21
  cartels, 21–22
  costs under, 23
  empirical studies re, 26–27
  inter-firm agreements, 22
  legal, 1, 27–29
  market supply restrictions through, 20–21
  misallocation of resources and, 18, 22–23
  "monopolizing" distinct from, 39
  price discrimination and, 21
  product differentiation and, 31
  production increases through, 21

profitability and, 26–27
public perception of, 9–10
Standard Oil case, 23–26
technical inefficiency under, 22–23
traditional definition of, 17
Monopoly theory, 5, 9–10 (*see also* Barriers to entry)
  criticism of, vii
  errors of, 20–23, 26, 27
Mueller, Dennis, 27n
Mueller, Willard F., 33n

National Steel, 6
Nelson, Phillip, 37n
Non-signer clauses, 50–51

O'Driscoll, Gerald P., Jr., 73n
Output restrictions, 59, 64–66
Overstreet, Thomas R., 50n
Owen, Bruce M., 14

Pabst Brewing Company, 6
Parker doctrine, 29n
Pautler, Paul A., 59n
Peckham, Rufus W., 65
Peltzman, Sam, 10n
Petroleum-refining industry, 23–26, 43
Phillips, Almarin, 66n
Pilon, Roger, 69n
Plan-coordination theory of market efficiency, 73–74
Poole, Robert W., Jr., 15n
Popper, Andrew, 63n
Posner, Richard A., xn, 49n
Predatory practices, 4
  consumer support for, 42–43, 44
  examples of, 43–44
  inefficiency of, 43
  nonprice practices, 1, 41, 42–43
  price cutting, 41–42, 43
Price discrimination, 1
  Borden Company case, 47–48
  competitive process, role in, 45–46
  definition of, 45
  "good faith" discriminations, 46
  laws re, 45
  monopolies and, 21
  property rights and, 69–70
Price fixing, 4
  in cast-iron-pipe industry, 65–66
  efficiency through, 61–64

77

About the Author

Dominick T. Armentano is professor of economics at the University of Hartford, where he has taught since 1967. He has also taught at the University of Connecticut, where he received his Ph.D. in economics in 1966. In spring 1984 he was Shelby Cullom Davis Visiting Professor at Trinity College in Hartford, Connecticut. Armentano is the author of *The Myths of Antitrust: Economic Theory and Legal Cases* (Arlington House, 1972) and *Antitrust and Monopoly: Anatomy of a Policy Failure* (John Wiley, 1982). His essays and articles have appeared in many other books, including William P. Snavely's *Theory of Economic Systems* (Charles Merrill, 1969), Yale Brozen's *The Competitive Economy* (General Learning Press, 1975), and Louis M. Spadaro's *New Directions in Austrian Economics* (New York University Press, 1978). His shorter articles and reviews have appeared in such journals and newspapers as *Business & Society Review*, the *New York Times*, the *Wall Street Journal*, *Inquiry*, and the *Cato Journal*.

Cato Institute

Founded in 1977, the Cato Institute is a public policy research foundation dedicated to broadening the parameters of policy debate to allow consideration of more options that are consistent with the traditional American principles of limited government, individual liberty, and peace. Toward that goal, the Institute strives to achieve a greater involvement of the intelligent, concerned lay public in questions of policy and the proper role of government.

The Institute is named for *Cato's Letters*, pamphlets that were widely read in the American Colonies in the early eighteenth century and played a major role in laying the philosophical foundation for the revolution that followed. Since that revolution, civil and economic liberties have been eroded as the number and complexity of social problems have grown. Today virtually no aspect of human life is free from the domination of a governing class of politico-economic interests. A pervasive intolerance for individual rights is shown by government's arbitrary intrusions into private economic transactions and its disregard for civil liberties.

To counter this trend the Cato Institute undertakes an extensive publications program dealing with the complete spectrum of policy issues. Books, monographs, and shorter studies are commissioned to examine the federal budget, Social Security, regulation, NATO, international trade, and a myriad of other issues. Major policy conferences are held throughout the year, from which papers are published thrice yearly in the *Cato Journal*.

In order to maintain an independent posture, the Cato Institute accepts no government funding. Contributions are received from foundations, corporations, and individuals, and other revenue is generated from the sale of publications. The Institute is a nonprofit, tax-exempt, educational foundation under Section 501(c)3 of the Internal Revenue Code.

CATO INSTITUTE
224 Second St., S.E.
Washington, D.C. 20003